Coping with Stress

ISSUES
(formerly Issues for the Nineties)

Volume 32

Editor

Craig Donnellan

Independence
Educational Publishers
Cambridge

First published by Independence
PO Box 295
Cambridge CB1 3XP
England

British Library Cataloguing in Publication Data
Coping with Stress – (Issues Series)
I. Donnellan, Craig II. Series
155.9'042

ISBN 1 86168 142 9

Printed in Great Britain
The Burlington Press
Cambridge

Typeset by
Claire Boyd

Cover
The illustration on the front cover is by
Pumpkin House.

CONTENTS

Chapter One: Young People and Stress

Stress	1
Exams come top of the teenage worry charts	2
Exam stress	3
Scientists unlock the secret of exam nerves	3
Coping with exam results	4
Coping with exam stress	5
Anxiety and phobias	6
Young under more stress	8
Suicide fear for pupils under tests pressure	9
Stress, the dos and don'ts	9
Parents' long hours 'stressing children'	10

Chapter Two: Stress in the Workplace

Mental health in the workplace	11
Key facts on stress at work	13
Taking the strain	14
Stress	16
Stress at work	18
Stress – a few facts	19
Stress	21
Wound-up over work	23
Dealing with stress at work	24
Our family life is being ruined say stressed bosses	25
A problem shared . . .	26
Take it easy, it's only a job	27
Off sick with stress	28
Absence cost business £10 billion in 1999 – says survey	29
Rising stress brings 'desk rage' at work	30

Chapter Three: Coping With Stress

Learning to cope with stress	31
Flora facts – stress	32
Stress and anxiety	33
Women and stress	34
Stress and your heart	35
One-minute stress beaters	36
Eating your stress away . . .	38
What you can do	40
Additional resources	41
Index	42
Web site information	43
Acknowledgements	44

Introduction

Coping with Stress is the thirty-second volume in the **Issues** series. The aim of this series is to offer up-to-date information about important issues in our world.

Coping with Stress looks at the causes of stress and how it affects different people. Ways of coping with stress are also explored.

The information comes from a wide variety of sources and includes:
Government reports and statistics
Newspaper reports and features
Magazine articles and surveys
Literature from lobby groups
and charitable organisations.

It is hoped that, as you read about the many aspects of the issues explored in this book, you will critically evaluate the information presented. It is important that you decide whether you are being presented with facts or opinions. Does the writer give a biased or an unbiased report? If an opinion is being expressed, do you agree with the writer?

Coping with Stress offers a useful starting-point for those who need convenient access to information about the many issues involved. However, it is only a starting-point. At the back of the book is a list of organisations which you may want to contact for further information.

*****

Stress

Information from the Royal College of Psychiatrists

What is stress?

Everyone feels stressed at times, however young or old they are. We feel under pressure, worried, upset, sad, angry . . . or maybe a mixture of uncomfortable feelings. It's usually because things in our life are difficult, or because we aren't getting on well with other people. Most of these stressful things last only a short time – then they get sorted out.

There are many ordinary situations that can make you feel stressed for a longer time. Your school work can pile up, or preparing for exams can seem like it's taking forever. At school you may be teased or bullied, or have problems with teachers. At home you may have arguments with parents, brothers or sisters, or close friends.

Stress can be even worse if you are hit a lot or sexually abused, or see your parents fighting. It can be particularly upsetting if your family is breaking up, or someone close to you is ill, or dies.

The effects of stress

This depends on how severe the stress is and how long it goes on for. It also depends a lot on the individual. We all react in different ways to stress. How you deal with it depends on your personality and on how well you've learnt to cope with things. It also depends on whether you've got someone you trust to talk to. Understanding and support from other people makes it much easier to cope with stress. Feeling alone makes it harder.

Stress can affect you physically. Your body is designed to be able to cope with stresses such as danger, illness and emergencies. Adrenalin, cortisol and other hormones help to gear your body up for 'fight or flight'. Your body is less well adapted to cope with longer-lasting pressure.

This can make you feel tired, make you go off your food and mess up your sleep. You may get stomach-aches or headaches.

Stress can affect you mentally as well as physically. It's harder to keep your mind on your work and harder to solve problems. It's more difficult to cope with frustration and control your temper. You might get depressed.

Stress that goes on for a long time can be exhausting, and can even make you ill.

Coping with stress

There are several things that you can do to help yourself cope. For things that happen every day, it can be useful to think of your stress as a puzzle to be solved:
- Work out the situations that stress you, and how you behave.
- Work out how you could behave differently in these situations, so that you feel more in control of them.
- Imagine how other people might behave if you acted differently.

- Rehearse some of these different ways of behaving. It might be a bit embarrassing, but try doing it out loud with a friend.
- Be prepared to fail the first time you try it out in real life – but be prepared to try again!
- List all the things you can think that would make things easier or less stressful – write them down on a piece of paper.

Finding the best solutions

Ask yourself: 'Do I feel comfortable about handling the situation this way? And will it get me what I want?' For example, if you don't do your school work, you may feel less stressed for a while – but you'll also find it hard to get into college or to get a decent job.

Ask yourself: 'Is there another way of dealing with the problem which will work better for me than the one I usually use?'

Thinking like this can be useful even when you are faced with less common situations, like being bullied, being offered drugs, involved

in the start of a fight with a friend, or being threatened on the street. For these really tricky situations, it's even more important to rehearse what you're going to say and how you're going to behave.

If it's hard to decide what to do, try sharing your ideas with your friends or family. It can help if you make a list of the advantages and disadvantages of each approach to help you decide which one to use.

If you can't cope, get help

Sometimes stress gets on top of you. Especially when the situation causing the stress goes on and on, and the problems just seem to keep building up. You can feel quite trapped, as if there is no way out and no solution to your problems. If you feel like this, it is important to get help.

People you might want to talk to could be:

- parents, a family member or family friend.
- a close friend.
- a school nurse, teacher or school counsellor.
- a social worker or youth counsellor.
- a priest, someone from your church or temple.
- the Samaritans (telephone 0345 90 90 90).

Your family doctor or practice nurse may also be able to help. They may suggest that you see someone from your local child and adolescent mental health service – a team of professionals specially trained to work with young people. They include child and adolescent psychiatrists, psychologists, social workers, psychotherapists and specialist nurses. They will respect your wishes about confidentiality and about the type of help you would like.

Get help if . . .

- You feel that stress is affecting your health.
- You feel so desperate that you think about stopping school, running away, taking an overdose or cutting yourself.
- You feel low, sad, tearful, or feel that life is not worth living.
- You lose your appetite and find it difficult to sleep.

- You have worries, feelings and thoughts that are hard to talk about because you feel people won't understand you or think you 'weird'. Stress may be making you hear voices telling you what to do, or make you behave strangely. You may be depressed. If so, it is very important that you get specialist help as soon as possible. Your doctor will be able to help.

Sources of further information

ChildLine provides a free and confidential service for children. ChildLine, Freepost 1111, London N1 0BR. Telephone 0800 1111. Website www.childline.org.uk

The Samaritans provide a 24-hour service offering confidential emotional support to anyone who is in crisis. Telephone helpline 0345 90 90 90.

Youth Access offers information, advice and counselling throughout the UK. 19 Taylor's Yard, 67 Alderbrook Road, London SW12 8AB. Telephone 020 8772 9900.

The YoungMinds Parent Information Service provides information and advice on child mental health issues. 102-108 Clerkenwell Rd, London EC1M 5SA. Telephone 0800 018 2138.

The *Mental Health & Growing Up* series contains 36 factsheets on a range of common mental health problems, including discipline, behavioural problems and conduct disorder, and stimulant medication. To order the pack, contact Book Sales at the Royal College of Psychiatrists, 17 Belgrave Square, London SW1X 8PG. Telephone 020 7235 2351, fax 020 7245 1231; e-mail booksales@rcpsych.ac.uk.

Exams come top of the teenage worry charts

Pupils are under intolerable pressure to do well in exams and get a good job, research revealed yesterday.

Many parents push their children into a cycle of worry, according to the survey.

Almost half the teenagers questioned admitted to losing sleep because of their worrying and two-thirds described themselves as 'worriers'.

One in five said they were permanently pessimistic.

The teenagers said that seven in ten parents became more strict as exams approached.

Exams are the leading worry for teenagers, with eight in ten putting them at the top of their 'worry list'. Fear of unemployment was second. The second annual analysis of teenage anxieties was carried out for publishing group Collins.

Child stress expert Gael Lindenfield said: 'Parents need to do whatever they can do to help.'

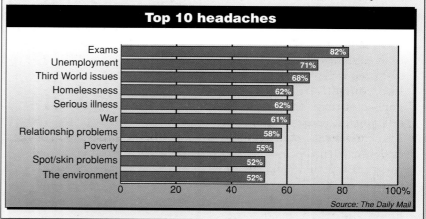

Top 10 headaches

Worry	%
Exams	82%
Unemployment	71%
Third World issues	68%
Homelessness	62%
Serious illness	62%
War	61%
Relationship problems	58%
Poverty	55%
Spot/skin problems	52%
The environment	52%

Source: The Daily Mail

Exam stress

Information from ChildLine

Dos

- Try to work to a revision timetable – start planning well before exams begin – your teacher should be able to help you with this.
- Make your books, notes and essays more user-friendly with summary notes, headings, sub-headings, highlighting and revision cards. Try using key words or spider charts. Get tips on other revision techniques from teachers and friends – do what works for you.
- Everyone revises differently – find out what routine suits you best – alone or with a friend; morning or late at night; short, sharp bursts or longer revision sessions.
- Take notes of important points when revising as an aid for future revision or if you need to clarify something with a teacher. Try explaining the answers to tricky questions to someone else, or look at past exam papers and try answering some of the questions.
- Ask for help if there are things you don't understand. If you're feeling stressed out, talk to someone.

Don'ts

- Don't leave revision to the last minute.
- Don't avoid revising subjects you don't like or find difficult.
- Don't forget that there is a life beyond revision and exams.
- Don't cram ALL night before an exam.

Pamper yourself

- Remember it's important to eat and sleep well.
- Put yourself first, it is an important time for you – try to talk to your family about how they can make studying a little easier for you, e.g. by agreeing times when you can have your own space, when they will try to be a little quieter around the house and when you'd rather not be disturbed (except perhaps for the occasional treat such as a drink or snack).

Don't revise all the time. Take breaks to do things you enjoy and help you relax.

Prepare for the big day

Check . . .
- Have a good breakfast if you can.
- Give yourself plenty of time to get to the exam room.
- Make sure you know where the exam is being held.
- Take everything you will need – extra pens, water, tissues – anything else?
- Go to the loo before the exam starts!

If you feel really anxious, breathe slowly and deeply while waiting for the exam to start.

Pace yourself

- Read the instructions – ask the teacher or invigilator if anything seems unclear – don't panic!
- Read all of the questions, twice if necessary, and give yourself time to answer those you are required to do.
- Plan how much time you'll need for each question.
- If you're stuck on a question, go on to the next. You can always come back to the unfinished one later. If you're really stuck, try to have an intelligent guess anyway.
- Leave time to read through and check your answers before the exam finishes.

Perform as well as you can

- You're you, so you can only do the best that you can on the day.
- Knowing that you've done your best on the day may help you overcome feelings of letting anyone down.
- Don't go through the answers afterwards with your friends if it is only going to make you more worried.
- Try to put the last exam out of your mind and look ahead to the next one – you can't go back and change things.

Scientists unlock the secret of exam nerves

By Tim Radford, Science Editor

Psychiatrists think they have found out why some people's minds go blank the moment they see an exam paper. Blame it on the stress hormone cortisol, which jams the memory.

Researchers at Zurich University took 36 people and asked them to memorise 60 German nouns, the journal *Nature Neuroscience* reports. They asked them to recall the words immediately and then 24 hours later.

That set the 'normal' performance level. Then the researchers piled on the stress by giving some of the volunteers cortisone, which turns to cortisol. None of the subjects felt stressed – cortisol is a product of stress and not its cause – but the result was the same as if they had experienced exam nerves. The cortisone tablets affected the recall of words 24 hours after they were shown.

© Guardian Newspapers Limited, 2000

Phew!

- Exams over? – pat yourself on the back – it's time to relax and forget about them.
- If you did well – Congratulations!

But . . .

- Remember, there's life beyond exam results. Disappointing results are not the end of the world – even if it does feel that way at the time. You might decide to resit, and there'll be lots of other opportunities to express yourself and succeed later on in life.

Don't bottle it up!

During or after the exams, if you feel that you can't cope with the pressure, or are feeling stressed, find someone to talk to – don't bottle it up!

Try to talk to parents, teachers, friends, or call ChildLine free of charge and in complete confidence on 0800 1111, or write to ChildLine, Freepost, London N1 0BR

Good luck!

Parents only!

- Give encouragement, not pressure.
- Give your support, not criticism.
- Make it easier for your child to study.
- Keep things in perspective.
- Get advice from the experts if you're worried.
- Exams are important – but they are not the only key to a successful future.   © ChildLine

Coping with exam results

Information from The Samaritans

Waiting for exam results is a unique kind of stress. So is receiving the results. Panic, anxiety, fear about the future, guilt, despair, these are just some of the feelings that you might be going through. Anyone coping with this stressful time needs a great deal of emotional support, but asking for help is not always easy. Without anyone to confide in, stress, anxiety and fear can be unbearable. High expectations from parents, teachers or friends can push you to the brink, particularly when you feel your results don't quite meet those expectations.

The first step is to recognise that you are suffering from stress.

How do you feel?

- Are you angry and impatient with people close to you?
- Do you feel close to tears over small events?
- Are you behaving differently from usual?

- Do you feel isolated from people around you?
- Is your self-esteem at rock bottom?

Do you have any of these physical symptoms?

- Sleeplessness
- Loss of appetite or irregular eating
- Panic attacks and difficulty breathing
- Tight, knotty feelings in your stomach
- Low energy and lack of concentration
- Loss of interest in things around you.

What can you do about it?

- Talk to someone you trust, whether that is a friend, teacher or relative
- Eat healthy food regularly
- Get exercise – walking, running, dancing, sport
- Get a reasonable amount of sleep.

Why does talking help?

Talking openly about how you really feel can be like opening a door. Talking puts you back in control and reveals the choices you have. Many people feel pressured into hiding their feelings out of embarrassment or concern not to burden family or friends.

But hiding under a calm exterior only saves the problem for later and stress can build up until it becomes unbearable. Don't leave it that long. Remember your emotional health is your responsibility and The Samaritans is there to help whatever time of the day or night. You can call a Samaritan 24 hours a day on 0345 90 90 90 (UK) or 1850 60 90 90 (Republic of Ireland) to talk through stress, depression or anxiety, in total confidence. You can also e-mail The Samaritans on jo@samaritans.org.

If you know someone in distress, encouraging them to phone or e-mail The Samaritans will help them take their first step. Good luck.

© The Samaritans

Coping with exam stress

Information from the International Stress Management Association (UK)

General exam stress-busting tips

Believe in yourself
You wouldn't have been given a place on the course if you didn't have the ability to do it. Therefore, if you prepare for the exams properly you should do fine, meaning that there is no need to worry excessively.

Don't try to be perfect
It's great to succeed and reach for the stars. But keep things in balance. If you think that 'anything less than A+ means I've failed' then you are creating mountains of unnecessary stress for yourself.

Aim to do your best but recognise that none of us can be perfect all of the time.

Take steps to overcome problems
If you find you don't understand some of your course material, getting stressed out won't help. Instead, take action to address the problem directly by seeing your course tutor or getting help from your class mates.

Don't keep things bottled up
Confiding in someone you trust and who will be supportive is a great way of alleviating stress and worry.

Keep things in perspective
The exams might seem like the most crucial thing right now, but in the grander scheme of your whole life they are only a small part.

Tips for the revision period

Leave plenty of time to revise so that you don't get into a situation of having to do last minute cramming. This approach will help to boost your confidence and reduce any pre-exam stress as you know you have prepared well.

Develop a timetable so that you can track and monitor your progress. Make sure you allow time for fun and relaxation so that you avoid burning out.

As soon as you notice your mind is losing concentration, take a short break. You will then come back to your revision refreshed.

Experiment with several alternative revision techniques so that revision is more fun and your motivation to study is high.

Don't drink too much coffee, tea and fizzy drinks; the caffeine will 'hype' you and make your thinking less clear. Eat healthily and regularly; your brain will benefit from the nutrients.

Regular moderate exercise will boost your energy, clear your mind and reduce any feelings of stress.

Try out some yoga, tai chi or relaxation techniques. They will help to keep you feeling calm and balanced, improve your concentration levels and help you to sleep better.

Tips for the exam itself

Avoid panic. It's natural to feel some exam nerves prior to starting the exam, but getting excessively nervous is counterproductive as you will not be able to think as clearly.

The quickest and most effective way of eliminating feelings of stress and panic is to close your eyes and take several long, slow deep breaths.

Breathing in this way calms your whole nervous system. Simultaneously you could give yourself some mental pep-talk by mentally repeating 'I am calm and relaxed' or 'I know I will do fine'.

If your mind goes blank, don't panic! Panicking will just make it harder to recall information. Instead, focus on slow, deep breathing for about one minute. If you still can't remember the information then move on to another question and return to this question later.

After the exam don't spend endless time criticising yourself for where you think you went wrong. Often our own self-assessment is far too harsh.

Congratulate yourself for the things you did right, learn from the bits where you know you could have done better, and then move on.

• These tips were produced for ISMA by Dr Dawn Hamilton. If you wish to go into the subject in more detail then you should read her excellent book *Passing Exams – A Guide for Maximum Success and Minimum Stress* by Dawn Hamilton PhD, published by Cassell, ISBN 0-304-70489-X

Anxiety and phobias

Information from the Royal College of Psychiatrists

Introduction

Anxiety is a normal human feeling. We all experience it when faced with situations we find threatening or difficult.

People often call this feeling stress but the word 'stress' can be used to mean two different things – on the one hand, the things that make us anxious and on the other, our reaction to them. This makes it a confusing word and so it will not be used in this article.

When our anxiety is a result of a continuing problem, such as money difficulties, we call it worry, if it is a sudden response to an immediate threat, like looking over a cliff or being confronted with an angry dog, we call it fear.

Normally, both fear and anxiety can be helpful, helping us to avoid dangerous situations, making us alert and giving us the motivation to deal with problems. However, if the feelings become too strong or go on for too long, they can stop us from doing the things we want to and can make our lives miserable.

A phobia is a fear of particular situations or things that are not dangerous and which most people do not find troublesome.

Symptoms

Anxiety

In the mind:
- Feeling worried all the time
- Feeling tired
- Unable to concentrate
- Feeling irritable
- Sleeping badly

In the body:
- Irregular heartbeats (palpitations)
- Sweating
- Muscle tension and pains
- Breathing heavily
- Dizziness
- Faintness
- Indigestion
- Diarrhoea

These symptoms are easily mistaken by anxious people for evidence of serious physical illness – their worry about this can make the symptoms even worse. Sudden unexpected surges of anxiety are called panic, and usually lead to the person having to quickly get out of whatever situation they happen to be in. Anxiety and panic are often accompanied by feelings of depression, when we feel glum, lose our appetite and see the future as bleak and hopeless.

Phobias

A person with a phobia has intense symptoms of anxiety, as described above. But they only arise from time to time in the particular situations that frighten them. At other times they don't feel anxious. If you have a phobia of dogs, you will feel OK if there are no dogs around, if you are scared of heights, you feel OK at ground level, and if you can't face social situations, you will feel calm when there are no people around.

A phobia will lead the sufferer to avoid situations in which they know they will be anxious, but this will actually make the phobia worse as time goes on. It can also mean that the person's life becomes increasingly dominated by the precautions they have to take to avoid the situation they fear. Sufferers usually know that there is no real danger, they may feel silly about their fear but they are still unable to control it. A phobia is more likely to go away if it has started after a distressing or traumatic event.

Are they common?

About one in every ten people will have troublesome anxiety or phobias at some point in their lives. However, most will never ask for treatment.

Causes

Some of us seem to be born with a tendency to be anxious – research suggests that it can be inherited through our genes. However, even people who are not naturally anxious can become anxious if they are put under enough pressure.

Sometimes it is obvious what is causing anxiety. When the problem disappears, so does the anxiety. However, there are some circumstances that are so upsetting and threatening that the anxiety they cause can go on long after the event. These are usually life-threatening situations like car crashes, train crashes or fires. The people involved can feel nervous and anxious for months or years after the event, even if they have been physically unharmed. This is part of what we now call post-traumatic stress disorder.

Sometimes anxiety may be caused by using street drugs like amphetamines, LSD or Ecstasy. Even the caffeine in coffee can be enough to make some of us feel uncomfortably anxious!

On the other hand, it may not be clear at all why a particular person feels anxious, because it is due to a mixture of their personality, the things that have happened to them, or life-changes such as pregnancy.

Seeking help

If we are put under a lot of pressure, we may feel anxious and fearful for much of the time. We usually cope with these feelings because we know what is causing them and we know when the situation will end. For instance, most of us will feel very anxious before taking a driving test, but we can cope because we know that the feelings will disappear once the test is over.

However, some of us have these feelings for much of the time without knowing what is causing them, and so not knowing when they might end. This is much harder to cope with and will usually need some help from somebody else. People will sometimes not want to ask for help because they think that people might think that they are 'mad'. In fact, people with anxiety and fears hardly ever have a serious mental illness. It's much better to get help as soon as you can rather than suffer in silence.

People with anxiety and phobias may not talk about these feelings, even with family or close friends. Even so, it is usually obvious that things are not right. The sufferer will tend to look pale and tense, and may be easily startled by normal sounds such as a door-bell ringing or a car's horn. They will tend to be irritable and this can cause arguments with those close to them, especially if they do not understand why the sufferer feels that they cannot do certain things. Although friends and family can understand the distress caused by anxiety, they can find it difficult to live with, especially if the fears seem unreasonable.

Anxiety and phobias in children

Most children go through times when they feel very frightened about things. It's a normal part of growing up. For instance, toddlers get very attached to the people who look after them. If for any reason they are separated from them, they can become very anxious or upset. Many children are scared of the dark or of imaginary monsters. These fears usually disappear as a child grows older, and they do not usually spoil the child's life or interfere with their development. Most will feel anxious about important events like their first day at school, but they stop being frightened afterwards and are able to get on and enjoy their new situation.

Teenagers may often be moody. They tend to be worried about how they look, what other people think of them, how they get on with people in general, but especially about how they get on with the opposite sex. These worries can usually be dealt with by talking about them. However, if they are too strong other people may notice that they are doing badly at school, behaving differently, or feeling physically unwell.

If a child or teenager feels so anxious or fearful that it is spoiling their life, it's a good thing to ask the family doctor to look into it.

Helping people with anxiety and phobias

Talking about the problem

This can help when the anxiety comes from recent knocks, like a spouse leaving, a child becoming ill or losing a job. Who should we talk to? Try friends or relatives whom you trust, whose opinions you respect, and who are good listeners. They may have had the same problem themselves, or know someone else who has. As well as having the chance to talk, we may be able to find out how other people have coped with a similar problem.

Self-help groups

These are a good way of getting in touch with people with similar problems. They will both be able to understand what you are going through, but may be able to suggest helpful ways of coping. These groups may be focused on anxieties and phobias, or may be made up of people who have been through similar experiences – women's groups, bereaved parent's groups, survivors of abuse groups.

Learning to relax

It can be a great help to learn a special way of relaxing, to help us control our anxiety and tension. We can learn these through groups, through professionals, but there are several books and videotapes we can use to teach ourselves. It's a good idea to practise this regularly, not just when we are in a crisis.

Psychotherapy

This is a more intensive talking treatment which can help us to understand and to come to terms with reasons for our anxieties that we may not have recognised ourselves. The treatment can take place in groups or individually and is usually weekly for several weeks or months. Psychotherapists may or may not be medically qualified.

If this is not enough, there are several different kinds of professionals who may be able to help – the family doctor, psychiatrist, psychologist, social worker, nurse or counsellor.

Medication

Drugs can play a part in the treatment of some people with anxiety or phobias.

The most common tranquillisers are the valium-like drugs, the benzodiazepines (most sleeping tablets also belong to this class of drugs). They are very effective at relieving anxiety, but we now know that they can be addictive after only four weeks' regular use. When people try to stop taking them they may experience unpleasant withdrawal symptoms which can go on for some time. These drugs should be only used for short periods, perhaps to help during a crisis. They should not be used for longer-term treatment of anxiety.

On the other hand, antidepressants are NOT addictive and can help to relieve anxiety as well as the depression for which they are usually prescribed. Some even seem to have a particular effect on individual types of anxiety. One of the draw-backs is that they usually take 2 to 4 weeks to work and some can cause drowsiness, dizziness, dry mouth and constipation. Taking a certain kind of antidepressant, the MAOIs, may mean that you have to stick to a special diet.

© Royal College of Psychiatrists
February, 2000

Young under more stress

By David Brindle, Social Services Correspondent

As many as one in five children and teenagers suffers mental health problems, according to a study published today.

Youngsters are coming under mounting stress at home and school, according to the study. Academic pressure, family break-ups and parental safety fears over outdoor play and after-school activities are all contributing to mental disorders.

Relationship problems are another cause of rising anxiety and the main factor in suicide attempts. They will be the focus of a new youth campaign to be unveiled next week by the Samaritans and Relate, the relationship counselling charity.

Young women aged 15-19 represent the highest single risk group for attempted suicide. Attempts by young men have almost tripled since the mid-1980s.

The study was commissioned by the Mental Health Foundation as part of a £1 million inquiry into the mental well-being of children and young people.

June McKerrow, the foundation's director, said children were 'failing to thrive emotionally'. Society needed to make a fundamental shift in attitude to promote mental health among the young.

'Great emphasis is placed on academic achievement, child safety and physical development, whilst emotional literacy is being neglected,' Ms McKerrow said.

The inquiry, *Bright Futures*, yesterday published a report drawing together all the main existing research on mental problems among young people, plus the evidence of more than 1,000 submissions from doctors, teachers, social workers and other professionals.

At any one time, the report says, 20 per cent of children and adolescents are suffering mental ill health and 10 per cent have problems sufficiently severe to require professional help. Some 8-11 per cent have difficulty getting on with their everyday lives.

Between the ages of four and 20, an estimated 12 per cent have diagnosable anxiety disorders, 10 per cent disruptive disorders, 5 per cent attention deficit disorder and 6 per cent developmental disorders, enuresis (bed-wetting) and substance misuse.

At any one time, the report says, 20 per cent of children and adolescents are suffering mental ill health

In the 16-19 range, 23 per cent are thought to have some form of mental health problem.

The report concludes that life has become much more competitive for children. Although we claim to be a child-centred society, it says, in many ways we exclude children and regard them as designer accessories or pampered pets.

'Despite the miles of pop psychology shelves in bookshops, the acres of daily psycho-journalism, and the hours of navel-gazing broadcasting, we are probably less able to stand in a child's shoes – certainly those of a troubled child – than many of our Victorian forebears were.'

Although the inquiry will not produce recommendations for action until later this year, it is already calling for earlier intervention to tackle mental health problems when children first exhibit them.

Earlier this week, the Government announced an investment of £84 million over three years in psychiatric services for the young.

John Hutton, junior health minister, said some of the money would be focused on inequities in services. 'We want to bring struggling and under-resourced services out of the doldrums.'

The initiative has been welcomed by YoungMinds, a mental health charity for children, which says it deals with hundreds of families unable to get services they need or facing long waiting lists.

Suicide fear for pupils under tests pressure

Parental and school expectations over the new examinations are causing neuroses even in four-year-old children

By Ben Russell, Education Correspondent

Children who suffer ever-increasing stress because of pressure to succeed from their families and schools could be driven to suicide, teachers warned yesterday.

Members of the Association of Teachers and Lecturers attacked the Government's drive to raise standards as 'factory farming', claiming pupils as young as four were exhibiting anxiety and neurosis because of 'intolerable pressure' imposed by national tests.

Hank Roberts, a teacher at Copland Community School in Wembley, north London, likened the state education system to that in Japan, where a record 192 children took their own lives last year.

He told the 150,000-strong union's annual conference in Belfast: 'The route this Government is treading is the route to child suicide like Japan because of the intolerable hothouse pressures put on children's learning. What's happened to play? What's happening to childhood?'

More than one in ten of the 780 children calling the children's charity ChildLine about exam stress last year were under 13. Some children told counsellors the stress was so great they had contemplated suicide.

Nearly two million children aged 7, 11 or 14 will take standard assessment tests (Sats) next month, as schools come under increasing pressure to meet the Government's targets for literacy and numeracy.

Mr Roberts blamed ministers, the Office for Standards in Education (Ofsted) inspectors, heads and classroom teachers. He said: 'What impact does this have on the pupils? The answer is it has a great and inevitable impact. The pressure to achieve is transmitted, the anxiety, the irritability, shortness of temper and all the other symptoms caused by stress.'

Peter Wilson, director of the mental health charity YoungMinds, said: 'For some children, testing is very demanding and distressing because they cannot do it. I would not say many of our children would go on to commit suicide, but there are now very significant mental health problems from many children who do not have the ability and readiness to take on this challenge.'

Estelle Morris, the School Standards minister, dismissed the

Stress, the dos and don'ts

By Ryan Alexander

Stress affects us all in different, sometimes unique ways. Stress will follow us throughout our lives and is more likely to increase before it decreases. So having established all this doom and gloom let's all just kill ourselves and be done with it – right? WRONG!

Knowing how to deal with stress is the solution. Realise that stress is an emotion that everyone has to encounter with no exceptions. Figures from the Health Education Authority (HEA) show:

Fact: One in four parents divorce with children under 16.

Fact: Every year 10,000 secondary school children lose a parent.

Fact: In any secondary school with 1,000 students, about 50 will be seriously depressed and 100 more will be experiencing significant mental distress.

Fact: One in 100 12-16-year-olds attempts suicide every year – equivalent to ten students in a school with 1,000 students.

Fact: 60 per cent of 11-24-year-olds turn to family and friends to help them cope with problems.

Fact: Only 5% believed alcohol could help to solve problems and just 2% said smoking or drug taking helped.

Fact: Young men are more likely to exercise as a way to relieve stress. I believe that 'prevention is better than cure'. With regard to school-related stress there are many practical ways that a person may prevent getting stressed.

Don't leave unfinished homework to pile up till Sunday evening.

Don't resort to drink and drugs as this will only cause more stress in the long run.

Don't take life too seriously. Things are never as bad as they seem.

Do get adequate amounts of sleep every night (average 8 hours).

Do sort out problems with teachers as they occur.

Do talk to someone you trust. A problem shared is a problem halved.

• The above is an extract from the youth magazine *Exposure*, produced by the Haringey Youth Project.

© Exposure Magazine

criticisms. She said: 'I'm not sure it's too much pressure to get children to read and write. I actually think children enjoy it. I do not accept the country is full of children who are incredibly anxious about their Sats after Easter.

'For ages we have put pressure on some of our 11-year-olds because they can't read and write. It does mean hard work, a bit more study on the part of the kids, but the bottom line is they go to secondary school with the basic skills they need.'

Teachers also passed a motion criticising Ofsted after the suicide of Pamela Relf, a Cambridgeshire primary school teacher. They called on Chris Woodhead, the chief inspector of schools, to reduce the stress of inspection. Andy Garner, from Suffolk, said: 'Pamela Relf's death is the tip of the iceberg when we discuss the victims of Ofsted.'

Delegates also criticised Mr Woodhead for his 'grudging and belated' expression of condolence after Miss Relf's death in January.

Parents' long hours 'stressing children'

By Rebecca Smithers,
Education Correspondent

One in five children suffers from a stress-related health problem as a result of Britain's 'long hours culture', a campaigner for a better deal for working parents claimed yesterday, as she urged parents and employers to achieve a healthier balance between work and home life.

The author Shirley Conran, chairwoman of Mothers in Management, called on Tony Blair to set an example to other working parents and take paternity leave when his fourth child is born at the end of May.

Ms Conran, who famously declared that 'Life is too short to stuff a mushroom' in her bestseller *Superwoman*, said it was time to put an end to the damaging long hours culture, in which achievement is measured in terms of employees' presence in the office – 'presenteeism' – rather than their output.

'The long hours culture threatens the health of everyone who practises it, and it has a domino effect on their families,' she said.

'One in five British children has a stress-related health problem. In the short term, industry might seem to gain from what is often unpaid labour, but firms refusing to address the stress problem will not be seen as employers of choice.'

Ms Conran is on a committee, headed by the education and employment minister Margaret Hodge, advising the government in its drive to encourage employers to introduce more balance to working life.

She is the former wife of the designer Sir Terence Conran, by whom she has two grown children.

Publishing a report, *Time bomb: why we need to change the way we work*, on the findings of a conference last year, Ms Conran said the issue of work/life balance was important enough to warrant the appointment of a minister to take charge of it.

> **'The long hours culture threatens the health of everyone who practises it, and it has a domino effect on their families'**

The report called for a change in attitudes in the workplace, with more flexible working options encouraged. These included proper flexitime, the choice of working at home when necessary, term-time working contracts, paid parental leave and a shorter working week. There should be tax relief on childcare for everyone and more workplace creches.

Ms Conran predicted that the prime minister would take paternity leave when the time came, but said his public dithering over the decision had simply made it a big issue. 'Of course he will take it. He must take it, in order to set an example to the rest of the country and as someone who clearly believes in the importance of family life.'

The report set out the ways in which 'downsizing', increased competition and insecurity, the pace of technological change and the growth of the 24-hour economy were combining to produce a workforce that felt 'stretched to its limits'.

It claimed that the burden of stress on all workers, and the knock-on effect on their families, had become an epidemic costing the national health service about £2bn every year and industry millions of lost working days a year.

The long hours culture presented 'a significant threat to the health of every individual that is caught up in it, as well as to the well-being of our children, the vitality of our communities and the state of our relationships'.

Sarah Jackson, chief executive of Parents at Work, said: 'Working parents and their children bear the brunt of the long hours culture. Parents at Work has long addressed the impact of long working hours on the family, through campaigning and practical support. We want a smart hours, not a long hours, culture.'

Mental health in the workplace

Information from the Mental Health Foundation

Introduction

Over 25 million people in the UK spend a large part of their lives at work. It stands to reason that a psychologically healthy workforce and a supportive work environment will benefit staff and employers alike. In a Confederation of British Industry (CBI) survey of over 800 companies, 98% of respondents said they thought that the mental health of employees should be a company concern. Similarly, the large majority (81%) considered that the mental health of staff should be part of company policy. Despite their concerns, however, less than 1 in 10 of these companies had an official policy on mental health.

The scale of the problem

Mental ill-health or distress is a major cause of sickness absence from work, reduced productivity and staff turnover. Stress is the root cause of a lot of mental ill-health, especially anxiety and depression.

- Work-related stress is estimated to be the biggest occupational health problem in the UK, after musculoskeletal disorders such as back problems.
- Nearly 3 in every 10 employees will have a mental health problem in any one year – the great majority of which will be anxiety and depressive disorders.
- Mental health problems account for the loss of over 91 million working days each year.
- Half of all days lost through mental ill-health are due to anxiety and stress conditions.

Stress is a necessary part of everyday life. Indeed, some degree of stress or pressure is considered healthy. Under-employment can lead to boredom, apathy and a loss of energy and motivation. But conversely, excessive stress can lead to fatigue, impaired judgement and decision making, exhaustion and the onset of serious health problems – both mental and physical.

Physically, stress is implicated in the development of coronary heart disease, certain types of cancer, and a host of other ailments including stomach ulcers, skin rashes, migraine, asthma, and increased susceptibility to infections.

The psychological effects of stress can be just as damaging. Increased anxiety, irritability, disturbed sleep, poor concentration and aggressive behaviour can increase the risk of accidents and disrupt relationships both at work and at home. Individuals under stress are often inclined to smoke more, drink more alcohol, and consume excessive amounts of caffeine, thus increasing irritability, sleep impairment, etc., in a vicious circle.

Exposure to prolonged stress will increase the risk of serious mental health problems, including depression and disabling anxiety conditions, as well as alcohol misuse.

Who is at risk?

Anyone can experience stress from their work, depending on the demands of their job, the conditions in which they work, and their individual susceptibility, which can be increased by problems outside of the workplace. In a recent research survey of 270 company line managers, 88% claimed a moderate or high level of stress in their work, which 39% claimed had got worse over the past year. Just over three-quarters of those surveyed – 77% – thought stress in the workplace 'will happen to everybody at some time'. Moreover, 52% said they knew someone who had suffered stress severe enough to stop them working and require long-term medical treatment.

The cost of mental ill-health

Mental ill-health among the workforce exerts a substantial cost from British industry.

- Stress-related sickness absences cost an estimated £4 billion annually.
- Lost employment constitutes 37% of the total cost of mental ill-health in England (£11.8 billion).
- The CBI estimates that 30 times as many days are lost from mental ill-health as from industrial disputes.

There are many other costs in addition to those of sickness absence. Ineffective working and poor interpersonal relations can substantially reduce productivity. Increased staff turnover necessitates recruitment costs. Administrative as well as personal costs are involved in covering for absent employees. Additional costs are incurred when staff take early retirement or medical severance on health grounds.

What can give rise to stress at work?

Work on the whole has a beneficial impact on mental health. It gives structure and purpose to the week, opportunities to meet people and make friends, and a means of increasing one's sense of self-worth and of being valued by others.

In certain circumstances, however, work can cause or contribute to stress and subsequent problems of anxiety and depression. Research has highlighted a number of work-related factors that can negatively affect well-being.

- Lack of control over work
- Under-utilisation of skills
- Too high a workload, impossible deadlines
- Too low a workload, no or few challenges
- Low task variety
- High uncertainty, e.g. due to poorly defined roles and responsibilities, lack of clear priorities and targets, job insecurity
- Low pay
- Poor working conditions, e.g. noise, overcrowding, excessive heat, inadequate breaks
- Low interpersonal support, e.g. via inadequate or insensitive management, hostility from colleagues
- Undervalued social position.

No single factor alone is likely to be the cause of someone becoming stressed at work. Stress tends to build up over a period of time through a combination of circumstances, some of which may not be related to work at all. Problems in domestic relationships, money worries, even difficulties in travelling to work can contribute to reducing a person's ability to cope with stress in the workplace.

If sufficient numbers of staff are affected by stress, however, the problem can become a serious organisational one, manifesting as absenteeism, reduced productivity, increased staff turnover and customer complaints. This becomes a particular risk during times of organisational change, such as restructuring or downsizing, which need to be anticipated and effectively managed if large numbers of staff are not to become disaffected.

The early warning signs

Most people will experience aspects of stress at work sometimes, and no employer can totally prevent this. However, when an individual or group of employees becomes so chronically stressed that their health and functioning are affected, there will usually be characteristic signs and symptoms. Any of the following can provide clues that something is wrong and an employer needs to take appropriate action to help.

Indicators of individual stress

- Increase in unexplained absences or sick leave
- Poor performance
- Poor time-keeping
- Increased consumption of alcohol, tobacco or caffeine
- Frequent headaches or backaches
- Withdrawal from social contact
- Poor judgement/indecisiveness
- Constant tiredness or low energy
- Unusual displays of emotion, e.g. frequent irritability or tearfulness.

Indicators of group level stress

- Disputes and disaffection
- Increased staff turnover
- Increased grievances and complaints

These can all be signs that stress has built to such an extent that an individual may be in danger of developing more severe anxiety or depression. Effective help in the early stages can help to prevent long-term problems both for individuals and organisations. Clearly this needs to be sensitively handled or the intervention may exacerbate the problem. The emphasis should be on providing reassurance and giving the individual the opportunity to talk about how they are feeling and to seek help.

• The above is an extract from *Mental health in the workplace*, a leaflet produced by the Mental Health Foundation. See page 41 for address details.

Stress at work

The table below shows the increase in workers reporting working at high speed and to tight deadlines in various EU countries. The scale is 1-7.

Country	1991	1996	Change
Great Britain	3.35	3.91	0.56
Ireland	2.90	3.38	0.48
France	2.72	3.20	0.48
Italy	2.45	2.87	0.42
Netherlands	3.18	3.60	0.42
Portugal	2.86	3.22	0.36
East Germany	3.66	3.89	0.33
Belgium	2.64	2.89	0.25
Spain	2.75	2.94	0.19
Luxembourg	2.64	2.81	0.17
Greece	3.51	3.58	0.07
Denmark	3.44	3.50	0.06
West Germany	3.44	3.47	0.03

Source: Green, F. and McIntosh, S. (2000) 'Working on the Chain Gang? An Examination of Rising Effort Levels in Europe in the 1990s,' Centre for Economic Performance, Discussion Paper no 465.

Key facts on stress at work

Information from the Institute of Personnel and Development (IPD)

Stress has become one of the most serious health issues of the 1990s and its impact is likely to continue well into the 21st century.

Many people are subjected to pressure when organisations take action to remain competitive. As organisations change and become more flexible, employees can be placed under considerable stress. It may not be possible to prevent stress associated with job insecurity and increases in work intensity, but an employer should control known causes such as:

- management style
- overwork through time available or lack of competence
- bullying and harassment
- adverse environments including excessive travel
- inadequate or inappropriate training.

Occupational health strategies will not succeed if they are regarded as peripheral activities. They need to be visibly supported by top management. Major initiatives which impact on work organisation need to take into account employee mental well-being. A systematic assessment of sources of stress and planning to mitigate these can help ensure stress reduction.

Background

The Health and Safety Executive defines work-related stress as 'the reaction people have to excessive demands of pressures, arising when people try to cope with tasks, responsibilities or other types of pressures connected with their jobs but find difficulty, strain or worry in doing so'.

'Not being able to cope' is a common denominator in other definitions of stress.

It is important to note that stress is not confined to managers, it is also common among manual workers.

Research evidence from the Institute of Personnel and Development has found that organisations with developed people management policies are more successful in the longer term. The concern of successful companies for employee welfare and development has been found to be a significant predictor of differences between the profitability and productivity of companies.

Aims

This summary:

- identifies stress as an increasingly serious health issue
- considers how stress influences business performance
- outlines legal responsibility in the light of recent judgements

---

Some key points

The price of stress

- A 1999 survey by the CBI found that employers reported workplace stress as the second most common cause of absence among non-manual employees.
- The Health and Safety Executive (HSE) estimates that 60% of all work absence is caused by stress-related illnesses, totalling 40 million working days per year.
- According to the HSE, 1 in 5 employees admit to taking time off work because of work-related stress and 1 in 13 consult their GP on stress-related problems.
- A 1997 survey by a long-term disability insurer found claims for compensation arising from mental problems had increased by 90% in the last five years.
- A 1996 survey on working conditions by the European Foundation for the Improvement of Living and Working Conditions showed that 28% of European workers consider their health is affected by stress at work. The Foundation's 1998 report found 'high stress' working conditions are on the increase in Europe with women suffering to a greater degree than men.

- provides an action plan to manage stress
- encourages review and sets stress reduction objectives.

Managing occupational stress

Signs and health consequences of stress

Stress causes complex changes in the body's chemical processes affecting the way people feel, think and behave. The immediate physical effects include a faster heart rate, a dry mouth and throat, butterflies in the stomach and excess perspiration. However, individuals react in different ways – some may hyperventilate, others may have headaches/migraine, muscle tension in their neck and shoulders, dizziness, blurred vision, skin rashes and allergies. Chronic stress can lead to physical and mental disorders.

Increases in colds and other infections as the immune system is weakened are early signs of stress. Other warnings could include backache and digestive illnesses. More serious conditions may follow such as ulcers, hypertension, angina and coronary heart disease. Heart attacks and increased susceptibility to tumour growth can be the ultimate consequences.

Fatigue seems a common reaction which is also related to difficulty in sleeping and insomnia. Other problems include anxiety, panic, irritability, hostility and aggression, psychosomatic complaints, depression and even 'nervous breakdowns'. Dealing with everyday tasks becomes daunting and consumption of alcohol, tranquillisers or tobacco increases as people under stress try to 'cope'. In terms of work, the end result may be 'job burn out' – when a person has depleted energy reserves, is pessimistic and dissatisfied, and has a low resistance to illness.

Sources of stress

Organisation culture and management style can be a source of stress.

Poor communications and indifferent leadership also create anxiety. Lack of competence causes stress too. This may arise from poor selection practices at the time of recruitment, promotion or transfer. It may arise because people have been inadequately trained for the new job. Social and economic events outside the employment relationship cause stress and need to be considered.

Lack of control and ambiguity in work is one of the main reasons for stress. According to the Department of Health's self-reported work-related illness survey in 1995, 46% of respondents declared that their stress-related illness was due to work overload, high pace, pressure of deadlines, too much responsibility

---

As organisations change and become more flexible, employees can be placed under considerable stress

---

and too little training. Other sources of stress included continual exposure to higher management, clients and customers; work which is repetitive or lacking in variety, fragmented or involving short cycles of activity. The work environment can also be a source of stress, due to noise, poor lighting or ventilation, physical isolation and poor ergonomics of VDUs and other equipment.

An important and often overlooked cause of stress is the failure of individuals to take responsibility for self-management of their learning and development and their consequent loss of confidence and inability to do the job. This also results in anxiety over their employability.

Trading and financial difficulties may bring a fear of redundancy or transfer and/or career stagnation which may lead to stress.

Poor relationships are major causes of stress. (Bullying, harassment and violence at work are not uncommon.) Other causes of stress include conflicting demands at work and home.

© *Institute of Personnel and Development*
September, 1999

Taking the strain

A survey of managers and workplace stress

Introduction
- The Institute of Management (IM), supported by PPP healthcare, has undertaken new research into stress management issues. The findings are presented in full in an IM research report and are summarised here.
- The objective of the research was to explore the impact of job-related stress among managers and to assess the extent of change or continuation from the earlier IM research studies into stress of 1993 and 1996.
- The latest IM survey sought to assess the extent of job-related stress among managers, identify organisational factors contributing to managerial stress, explore attitudes and beliefs about stress management and finally, to provide some practical guidance and recommendations.
- Research for the project was conducted in September 1999, when the views of 819 managers were obtained from a postal questionnaire sent to a random sample of 3,000 individual IM members. This represents a response rate of 27 per cent.

Background
- Achieving the right balance between too much and too little pressure has become an integral challenge of living and working in the new millennium.
- Pressure at work, however, can escalate over time to become stress which is damaging to both individuals and organisations. For the purposes of this report, work-related stress is defined as that which arises when the demands made upon individuals exceed, or appear to exceed, the resources available to manage those demands.
- The need to consider employees' well-being, and the possible costs of failing to do so, have made the issue of work-related stress an important one for UK employers. There has been a succession of high awards to employees based on claims for damages due to stress, particularly in the latter half of 1999 and early 2000.
- In national terms, the Health and Safety Executive has estimated that 90 million work days were lost in 1998 as a result of stress-related absence, at a cost of £5.2 billion.

- The effects of work-related stress for individuals can be detrimental in physical and behavioural terms. They are likely to have an impact upon people's private and working lives and upon employee morale, thus underlining the need for, and importance of, effective stress management and prevention.

Key findings
Managers at work
- The majority of managers know what they want to achieve (89 per cent) and look forward to going to work (50 per cent). However, they are often unhappy with the culture of their organisation (43 per cent), sometimes feel unable to cope with workloads (42 per cent) and struggle to meet goals and targets (40 per cent).
- Managers continue to work long hours despite increased awareness of the damaging impact of this practice. More than nine in ten work in excess of their contracted week. Nearly four in ten (37 per cent) work more than a 48-hour week. Almost half regularly take work home, and four in ten work at weekends.

- Today's managers work in a wide range of office environments. While 45 per cent have their own office, it is largely the preserve of senior management and chief executives (67 per cent). More than a quarter work open plan, and one in five shares with one or two colleagues.

The changing workplace

- Organisational changes have led to fundamental shifts for individuals and the way they work.
- The last year has seen nearly a quarter of organisations experience mergers or takeovers, while a third face the challenge of expanding into new markets.
- Within organisations nearly four in ten managers say they have introduced a programme to change the focus of activities, or the company culture. The continuing impact of new technology has driven change in 49 per cent of organisations.
- Sixty-nine per cent report increased workloads in the past year, with this figure rising significantly in organisations that have undergone delayering (77 per cent) or introduced new technology (76 per cent). Two-thirds of executives now have to handle an increase in responsibilities.

Direct impacts and pressure points

- Nearly three-quarters (72 per cent) of managers have received criticism from family or friends about their long hours of work. Nevertheless, 73 per cent claim that they had taken no time off at all during the previous year because of stress.
- Over a quarter (26 per cent) of managers currently feel they need some help in dealing with stress, compared with 21 per cent in 1996.
- The top three sources of stress, i.e. excessive pressure, for managers in the past 12 months are

time pressures and deadlines, constant interruptions and lack of adequate support.
- Over 70 per cent consider work-related stress to have adverse effects on their enjoyment of life, home life, work effectiveness and health.

Dealing with stress

- Over 8 per cent of respondents indicated that a stress audit had been conducted in their organisation in the last year.
- The most common ways for individual managers to deal with stress were to take more physical exercise, talk to family or friends, or consume alcohol.
- A quarter of managers would not know how or where to go for help, if needed, while 41 per cent say that there is not enough impartial advice and support available on dealing with stress.

Conclusions and recommendations

- This third survey of sources, perceptions and consequences of managerial work-related stress suggests that the levels revealed in 1993, considered at

that time to be unsustainable, and found to have worsened in 1996, have not lessened today.
- Many managers still experience unacceptable levels of work-related stress, feel unable to cope with their work, struggle to achieve targets and experience its adverse effects on their enjoyment of life.
- However, the survey findings suggest that many managers are not encouraged to promote actively or learn about the long-term benefits of managing stress.
- The research confirms that the culture of an organisation, the beliefs and attitudes held by its senior managers and the degree of concern for employee welfare that is communicated through example and practice, are all central to preventative stress management.
- Initiatives such as 360° appraisal, stress audits, internal employee satisfaction surveys, EAPs and internal communication audits are all useful tools in helping organisations identify possible problem areas and take appropriate action.
- At an individual level employees should learn to say no to excessive work demands, to manage their time productively and to have periods when they can work without being disturbed.
- It is possible however that some managers, while recognising the signs and symptoms of stress, feel unable to influence the causes. However by dint of their authority and position, managers, especially senior managers, are still best placed to address the issue of organisational stress.
- A climate of trust, open communications and genuine care will encourage individuals to be honest when they are losing the ability to cope.

© The Institute of Management
February, 2000

Issues causing managers stress

Sources of stress in the past 12 months:

Time pressure/deadlines	45%
Constant interruptions	38%
Lack of adequate support	37%
Incompetent senior management	37%
Poor internal communications	30%
Office politics	28%
Handling constant change	26%
Relationship with boss	25%
Too many internal meetings	24%
Securing access to the right information	23%
Unrealistic business objectives	22%
Keeping up with e-mails, voice mails	22%
Difficult work environment, e.g. open plan	20%
Lack influence	19%
Influx of new, untrained staff	18%
Dealing with customer complaints	17%
Making presentations	13%
Relationship with peers	9%

Source: Taking the Strain, Institute of Management

Stress

Information from PPP healthcare

What is it?

Stress is a part of life. We all experience some stress in response to pressures we may face from day to day. With too much, illness could develop. The word stress may have a double meaning as it is used to describe both the stimulus and its effect. It is more precise to talk about 'stressors' and 'stress responses', which can be either positive or negative, depending on their effect on well-being.

Social scientists have devised a list of life events and rated the relative stressfulness of each[1]. Thus: the death of a spouse rates 100 on the scale, whereas trouble with one's employer rates 23; being fired, 47; going to jail, 63; a change in sleeping habits, 16; getting divorced, 73. Whilst many stressful events in life are not high on this scale, their repetition has a disastrous cumulative effect.

How does it occur?

The most common stressor is the constant demand of varied interruptions whilst trying to carry on the usual routines of everyday life. This sounds familiar to most people.

The drain may take the form of impossibly high expectations from employers, spouses or perhaps the bank, and may be coupled with an increased feeling of loss of control over one's fate, leading to a decreased ability to cope and increased sense of being stressed.

The biggest stressors come from relationships with one's family household (parents, spouse, children), from the workplace, and from financial pressure.

Why does it occur?

As the body responds to stress, the heart beats faster, blood pressure rises, and other body systems prepare to meet the threat. When a person does something active to cope with a threat, these systems return to normal. Running away or fighting (the so-called fight-or-flight reaction) are both successful ways of coping with many physical threats.

Problems arise, however, when the body is prepared to cope with danger but cannot do so. Dealing with a difficult situation, for example, can cause the body to prepare for a fight-or-flight response, but when no action can be taken, the body's systems remain overactive. Similar repeated experiences of this frustrating nature can lead to a sense of being overloaded which is commonly called 'stress', but is more accurately called a 'negative stress response'.

Are certain people susceptible to stress?

Many factors may lead to stress-related disorders. Among these is a certain type of personality: 'type A', a term originally applied to people who are prone to coronary artery disease. The type-A coping style, characterised by competitive, hard-driving intensity, is common in Western 20th-century society, and mounting evidence indicates that type-A behaviour is associated with an increased incidence of several stress-related disorders.

Does stress make you ill?

In a classical and important study over 30 years ago researchers[2] found that bacterial throat infection causing illness was four times as likely

to occur after than before stressful events. This was confirmed in 1991[3] when a study showed that the rates of respiratory infections increased in line with increases in the degree of reported psychological stress. This experiment was performed under controlled circumstances and supports the idea that although exposure to infectious agents is necessary for illness, it is stress that in some way suppresses resistance, leaving individuals susceptible to physical illness[4].

Many other diseases such as high blood pressure, psoriasis, asthma, eczema, irritable bowel syndrome and a host of others can also be triggered and maintained by stress.

The importance of the meaning of life

If the total pressure of stressors is great enough, the essential meaning in life begins to fade. One study[5] showed that a sense of commitment and meaning was extremely important in protecting our health when we are under stress; another study[6] highlighted job satisfaction as the most important predictor for reports of low back pain; a further major report[7] showed that survival after life-threatening illness can depend heavily on whether we believe in what we are doing with our lives. In addition, other research[8] has shown that when we are older, how long we are likely to live depends most importantly on how much of what we're doing seems of value and has meaning. If a person starts to feel that life loses its meaning then something is seriously wrong in his or her life. It is important that the person is helped to recognise the dangers both to themselves and their family.

What effect does stress have?

The symptoms of a negative stress response have much in common with depressive illness, and indeed this itself may develop if the stressors remain unchanged. The mechanisms of coping fail, and the vital resource of hardiness is no longer enough to keep the person going. Illness develops.

Ten signs of rising stress

1. Disturbed sleep. Finding it hard to drop off to sleep; waking early; inability to get back to sleep.
2. Loss of pleasure in things once enjoyed.
3. Appetite changes. Eating far too much or too little.
4. Irritability and impatience. An increasingly short temper.
5. Tiredness, lack of energy even after a night's rest.
6. Inability to concentrate, meet deadlines or make decisions.
7. Loss of libido.
8. Increasing cynicism or loss of trust.
9. Anxiety and panic attacks.
10. Sense of losing control over events.

Ten ways to control stress

1. Reduce the stressors: cut out unnecessary tasks. Refuse to take on unnecessary chores.
2. Good personal time management and good communication within the family and workplace is a prerequisite for the ability to manage home and work demands.
3. Good communication with the family is a big help in cutting problems down to size. Share a problem and it will be halved.
4. Retain a sense of control over our lives and don't be overcome by feelings of helplessness.
5. Modify lifestyle: the use of alcohol, coffee, tobacco, food (especially chocolate) can lead to more problems; they give a false sense of comfort which is short-lived, and leads to increased craving for more of the same. These coping substitutes can also create new problems such as liver damage, increased anxiety, lung and heart disease and obesity, which feed on the stress and worsen the problem.
6. Non-prescribed or recreational drugs can give rise to serious addiction problems, but with huge increases in the scale of

craving and further problems. Never use mind-altering drugs to cope with stress.

7. Exercise and self-help relaxation techniques (yoga, transcendental meditation, self-hypnosis) can reduce the sense of being stressed and improve all the symptoms of stress. There is good scientific evidence that regular practice of self-help will reduce the risk of many different illnesses and diseases.
8. Up-to-date therapies such as CBT (Cognitive Behaviour Therapy) and psychotherapy can provide useful insights into the causes of one's stress, and equip a person to cope with the onset of stress symptoms.
9. Prescribed drugs can be helpful in the treatment of symptoms of stress, though not as a cure. They may help in controlling the very distressing effects of stress, such as phobias, panic attacks and so on.
10. Most importantly of all, to look after our own stress effectively, we must look after ourselves first. The aim is always to find a way to regain control of our lives.

References

1. *Microsoft Encarta Encyclopaedia* (1993-1995) Stress related disorders.
2. Meyer, R.L et al. (1962) Streptococcal infections in families *Paediatrics* 29 pp.539-549.
3. Cohn, S. et al. (1991) Psychological stress and susceptibility to the common cold *New England Journal of Medicine* 325, pp.606-612.
4. Ridsdale, L.(1995) *Critical reading for general practice.* London: W.B.Saunders.
5. Kobasa, S.C., Maddi, S.R. and Kahn, S. (1982) Hardiness and health: a prospective study *Journal of Personal and Social Psychology* 42 pp.168-177.
6. Bigos, S.J. et al. (1991) A prospective study of work perceptions and psychosocial factors affecting the report of back injury *Spine* 16 pp.1-6.
7. (1973) *Work in America: report of a special task force to the Secretary of State for Health.* Cambridge: MIT Press.
8. Palmore, E. (1969) Predicting longevity: a follow up controlling for age. *Gerontologist* 9 pp.247-250.

Stress at work

Information from the London Hazards Centre

Workers in the UK don't need to be told that work has got harder and become a pressure cooker for stress over recent years. Longer hours of work, low hourly rates of pay, under-staffing, bullying and job insecurity currently have some effect on most people's health. People at the lower end of the job hierarchy are, as ever, disproportionately affected. Insurers and solicitors are regularly holding seminars for employers on how to sack stressed workers before they become a financial burden or take out compensation claims. In this vicious climate Safety Representatives and trade unions must develop strategies to tackle this issue as members' health, jobs and careers are on the line. Stress is a health and safety issue not least because there is relevant legislation and case law, but also involves broader employment, representational and collective bargaining issues.

Causes and symptoms

Occupational stress arises when workers perceive that they cannot adequately cope with the demands made on them or with threats to their jobs and the circumstances in which they are carried out. The main factors which cause stress at work are lack of job security (threat of redundancy, short-term contracts, etc.), excessive workload (arising from inadequate staffing, long hours, unsatisfactory shift patterns), harsh supervision and discipline, lack of control over work organisation, and inadequate training and career prospects.

Stress can result in both health and behavioural problems. It can lead to stomach and heart disease and a variety of psychological illnesses. It is related to increased accident rates, relationship problems, absenteeism and drug and alcohol abuse. The most extreme effect of stress is sudden death, i.e. people work themselves to death. Many symptoms are transient and disappear when the source of stress is removed. But if stress is prolonged it can take longer to recover and permanent illness may result.

Legal requirements

Employers have a duty to safeguard the health and safety of employees under Section 2 of the 1974 Health and Safety at Work Act. Under Regulation 3 of the 1992 Management of Health and Safety at Work (MHSW) Regulations, employers are obliged to carry out an assessment of the risk in jobs and reduce these as far as possible. These legal duties apply to occupational stress so risk assessments must be done.

Safety Representatives operate under the 1978 Safety Representatives and Safety Committees Regulations which entitle them to, amongst other things, inspect the workplace, talk to fellow employees regarding health and safety issues, request a Safety Committee is set up and for it to meet regularly.

The new Health and Safety (Consultation With Employees) Regulations 1996 require employers to consult with workers where there isn't a recognised trade union on health and safety issues. They also allow for the appointment of Representatives of Employee Safety, a weaker version of the Safety Rep.

Case law on stress is contained in *Walker v. Northumberland County Council*. John Walker was a social worker who suffered two breakdowns related to his work. The employer took no action to modify his employment conditions upon his return to work after the first breakdown. The Court ruled that all the conditions of employer liability were present – breach of the duty of care, injury, causation and foreseeability. The employer appealed but eventually an out-of-court settlement of £175,000 in compensation was reached. In another out-of-court settlement, a social worker in Scotland received £66,000 after she was forced to retire through ill health caused by bullying by her superior. A supervisor employed by the Royal Ordnance who suffered post-traumatic stress illness after exposure to toxic fumes was awarded £125,000 in an out-of-court settlement.

Education and awareness

Workers do not need to be told that their jobs are stressful but may need to be persuaded that their health is at risk or that Safety Representative or union action can improve their conditions. Education is a two-way process, ensuring that workers are aware of the issues and what the union is doing about them, enabling representatives to find out what is happening in the workplace and to propose ways of tackling the problems. This can be done by:

- circulating leaflets, feature articles and posters on the hazards of stress
- carrying reports in local and national bulletins of union action to combat stress
- holding discussions at workplace or union meetings, perhaps with an invited speaker

- investigating key indicators of stress such as sickness absence figures
- conducting a survey of the incidence of stress among workers.

Confidentiality must be guaranteed in a survey and the results must be published. The survey should be one part of a broader plan of action whereby the union takes up the issue with the management.

Representing individual workers

The first priority is to protect the member's health and job where these are threatened by stress or by management responses. The second is to try and secure the solution the member wants. This could entail:
- ensuring behavioural problems are not treated as a disciplinary issue
- negotiating leave, a transfer or reallocation of work
- obtaining a second medical opinion if required
- resisting retirement on medical grounds or dismissal on grounds of inability to work
- helping the member get the right sort of professional assistance

pressing the management to remove or reduce the causes of stress.

Collective agreements

These can be of two types, an overall agreement aimed at eliminating or reducing stress or specific agreements on particular employment conditions. A general agreement would:
- recognise that stress is a health and safety issue and that employers have a duty to avoid it
- treat stress as a health issue where job performance is affected
- give priority to the assessment of jobs for their stress potential and for measures to eliminate or reduce it to a minimum
- provide counselling under conditions of strict confidentiality and which suit workers
- provide information and training for all employees.

The alternative is to negotiate anti-stress provisions into employment conditions such as staffing levels, working hours, shift patterns, performance levels, and all the variants of human resource management. The two approaches are not

incompatible. The introduction of health and safety considerations into general negotiations should help to strengthen the union's overall approach.

Traumatic incidents

Both short- and long-term disorders can arise in people exposed to traumatic incidents at work. Measures to assist workers in these circumstances should include:
- appropriate paid time off work
- availability of suitable counselling
- possibility of referral to specialist medical care.

Employer responses

Employer responses to occupational stress favour the provision of counselling, occupational health programmes, employee assistance programmes and healthy lifestyle campaigns. These may be helpful in reducing stress levels but they do not address the factors in the job which produce stress in the first place. They tend to transfer responsibility for the condition and its prevention from the employer to the individual worker.

© *London Hazards Centre*

Stress – a few facts

The scale of the problem

Stress is rapidly gaining recognition as one of society's most significant maladies. As the following startling statistics illustrate, employers and employees that ignore the issue, do so at their own peril.

Stress – the startling truth!
- The International Labour Office believes that stress has become one of the most serious issues of the 20th century, costing Britain up to 1% of Gross National Product.
- According to the Department of Health, 80 million work days are lost each year through emotional difficulties.
- Up to 25% of the workforce is affected by stress or more severe forms of mental illness.

- After colds and flu, stress is now the second largest category of occupational ill health, accounting for approximately 40% of sickness absence.
- 70% of GP surgery visits are for stress-related complaints.
- Stress costs the nation between £3.7 billion and £11 billion a year through sickness absence and health costs.
- Employers now have to pick up the cost for employee sickness – 40% of which is likely to be stress related.
- Department of Social Services statistics for 1991-92 show work days lost through stress related illness increased by 69.9% for men and 139.9% for women when compared with figures obtained between 1983-84.

- In 1995, a Price Waterhouse survey in the Midlands revealed one in six senior executives had time off work for stress-related illnesses. In the same survey where time had been lost to stress, nearly 34% of the illnesses lasted more than 10 working days, and 28% lasted between three and ten working days.

In sickness and ill-health
- Stress is not a tangible condition. This is a huge stumbling block in getting stress recognised as a genuine problem.
- Managers still have difficulty in accepting stress as an illness. Comments like 'stress is for wimps' and 'If you can't stand the heat . . . ' abound.

- In the 1995 Price Waterhouse survey, analysis suggests that the increased competitive pressures designed into the economy over the last 15 years, and the increase in the volume of work, are clearly damaging the health of senior executives.
- Research indicates that there is a link between stress and a number of major illnesses such as cancer and heart disease.
- One in four men will suffer heart disease before the age of 65 and one in twelve will die from it.
- As women adopt the lifestyles and responsibilities of men, they are becoming more prone to coronary heart disease than before.
- GPs increasingly ask about job anxieties when patients complain of backache or sexual problems.
- It has been estimated that at least 50% of headaches and stomach disorders are stress related.
- Exercise is a powerful way of eliminating stress hormones from the system. Good diet helps replace vitamins and minerals used during periods of stress. Relaxation lowers blood pressure and restores energy.
- A US corporation aware of stress issues introduced a counselling programme for employees. This resulted in a drop in absenteeism of 60% in one year, coupled with a 55% reduction in medical costs.
- The Post Office believes that stress is the second highest cause of medical retirement.
- Major symptoms of stress can include tiredness, irritability, headaches and insomnia. Depression and general anxiety also feature in survey responses.
- In Britain, three-quarters of a million people take tranquil-lisers of one form or another every single day.
- In 1994 a national Gallup poll revealed that of 1,014 'career' women, a third find work emotionally and physically exhausting.
- In 1995, Demos research revealed that stress, fatigue and general dissatisfaction are plaguing an increasing number of British employees who find that there are not enough hours in a day to both work and relax.
- In the face of threat (including stress), chemicals and hormones are released by the brain and the adrenal glands activating certain biological changes in the body. Under normal circumstances, when the threat has passed, the body regains its chemical and hormonal balance. However under unrelieved, prolonged stress, the biological imbalance associated with stress is not reduced and the immune system is put under strain.

Did you know?

- In 1995, the TUC said that two-thirds of 7,000 health and safety officers said that stress was their biggest concern.
- In 1996, out of 100 HR managers attending a conference, only 4% had a formal stress policy of some sort.
- Research by the IPD showed that many senior and middle managers were taking fewer holidays than they were entitled to because of work pressure.
- In more enlightened companies there has been a growth of American-style confidential counselling services.

- Demos research – The Time Squeeze revealed that working hours are longer in Britain than in the rest of Europe with 54% of managers working more than 50 hours a week.
- In 1995, research by Price Waterhouse revealed that the incidence of extreme stress in companies tends to be high where employment has declined sharply.
- In 1995, research by the Cranfield School of Management found that after a set of redundancies, those left behind suffered from 'survivor syndrome' – an apathy that may lead to poor perform-ance by the very employees who are being expected to be more productive.
- A 1995 CBI survey found that while 90% of companies considered that the mental health of their employees was vital to their competitive position, only 12% had a programme to deal with stress.
- Forward-thinking companies are now taking responsibility for encouraging preventative measures in their organisations. They find it makes good financial sense to help employees deal with stress before it causes absenteeism and poor productivity. Their interest and caring promotes a greater degree of loyalty and good service among employees.

Effects of stress

The effects of stress may be categorised into four areas.
- **Mental**. When experiencing excessive stress, employees are likely to have difficulty con-centrating, becoming forgetful, less rational and thinking less clearly. Under these circum-stances they may become in-decisive or take the wrong decisions. These effects are known to employers of people undertaking jobs that require vigilance and life-or-death decision-making, and who therefore monitor stress levels very carefully.
- **Emotional**. Mental ill health and absenteeism are both related to emotional reactions to stress.

In addition, employees may respond by becoming unduly aggressive or extremely irritable, which in turn affects relationships at home and work, and performance. These reactions to stress have the greatest impact when people have direct contact with customers, but are equally costly when employees have responsibility for others.

- **Behavioural signs**. The tendency to overwork is one factor. Employees also have difficulty working effectively when over-stressed and become obsessive about attending to trivia. They consequently miss important deadlines. People who are over-stressed also tend to smoke and drink more. Drink particularly impairs efficiency.
- **Effect on leadership**. Studies have shown that when under stress, managers resort to what has worked in the past rather than using their judgement. This is far less likely to be successful. Some individuals react badly in very stressful situations. For many years, organisations recruiting employees who will be required to react in life-threatening situations have screened out those who would fail to withstand the pressures. But care should be taken when recruiting to make sure particular groups are not discriminated against on the grounds that they might not be resilient. Decisions must be based on hard evidence.

(source *People Management* magazine)
© *International Stress Management Association (UK)*

Stress

Information from the Institute of Management

Introduction

Successive waves of downsizing, closures and reorganisations have created pressures for the managers of today. Technological changes to 'improve' communications such as mobile telephones, pocket pagers and answering machines have created twenty-four-hour accessibility. Today, there is no place to hide!

Organisations now often expect the same volume of work from fewer managers and employees. Some, in the short term, appear to cope with the pressures – even thrive under them. But stress has considerable costs. The detrimental effects on the organisation of poorly managed pressures show in terms of absentee-ism, inefficiency and quality. There is a real money cost to organisations and to the economy as a whole. For the UK, this is currently estimated to be about 40 million working days per year or £7bn.

For the individual, the effects of stress in terms of effectiveness and the quality of life are always harmful, and can sometimes be catastrophic. But many who are suffering the effect of too many demands are unwilling to admit they are being affected by these changes because of the fears that this will place their jobs in jeopardy.

Successful stress management is not an optional extra, it is an essential ingredient in ensuring the balance of work and career against family and health. Recognising the sources of pressures and developing strategies to prevent them or cope with them can be beneficial to all aspects of our lives. This checklist is devised to help managers understand their stress response and learn how to deal with the consequences in the short as well as the long term.

What is 'stress'?

'Stress' is a word firmly embedded in our vocabulary. In the course of a week it would not be unusual to hear stress used to describe a wide range of feelings, symptoms and situations:

'I feel stressed' – describing the rush and panic in meeting a deadline.

'They're under a lot of stress' – offered as an explanation for a colleague's unusual irritability or their un-characteristic behaviour.

'It's a stressful job' – awarding a specific job an odd status.

Pressures come from many different directions, and affect different people in different ways. The pressures which would cause serious stress in one individual might stimulate optimum achievement in another. Even for the same person, an event occurring at one time when, for example, they are physically unwell or tired, would cause more stress than the same event at another occasion. Sometimes we cope, are stimulated and positively thrive. At other times we may suffer, more or less seriously, and show signs of not coping and feel unable to meet either the deadlines or our expectations.

Stress, therefore, is a subjective experience. Its causes vary, and we must be alert above all to its effects, on ourself and on others.

The sources of stress

We live in an ever-changing world and must constantly adapt and adjust to both technological and social changes. In addition, there are recurring pressures which form a predictable pattern of events in our lives. Potentially, as with many other things, these may be both a source of stress and satisfaction.

Troubles often start when too many life events occur at once, as these can overtax our adaptive and coping resources. Life events such as the death of someone close, divorce, injury, a large mortgage and even happy events such as a holiday or marriage can all be stressful.

Some of these events such as illness are unpredictable and we have no control over them. Others are brought on by choice, such as taking out a large mortgage or moving house. Recognising the effects that life events have on us is central to our management of stress. We need to ensure that we do not overtax ourselves by creating unnecessary change in potentially turbulent times.

There are many aspects of the working environment that may contribute to stress:

- Overwhelming time pressures and demanding deadlines
- Relationships with others
- Too much work
- Business or work changes
- Threat of redundancy

As managers we do not manage in isolation. We have the responsibility for organisations, people, budgets, buildings or projects. Additionally work cultures and climates can have a profound effect on us – no one escapes the threat of the announcement of a major restructuring, closure of a site, relocation, redundancies, a merger or takeover. All these can present threats to our well-being and may result in stress.

Individuals respond to these external pressures, by adapting and adjusting in a variety of ways dependent on their lifestyle. However, other characteristics such as age, gender, health, financial situation and access to support can influence how we respond to change.

The symptoms

Stress manifests itself in our health, our behaviour and our work:

Our health

Our health can suffer from prolonged exposure to stress as the body believes it is preparing itself for immediate action – either to 'fight', in what may be a life-or-death struggle, or for the dash to safety – 'flight'. The body automatically releases adrenalin into the blood stream, shuts down the digestive system, thickens the blood so that it will clot and pumps blood more quickly around the body.

In the short term, this can lead to symptoms such as headaches, upset stomach, sleep problems, change in appetite, tense muscles, indigestion and exhaustion. However, long-term exposure to stress can have more serious consequences, as it can make us more vulnerable to stomach, intestinal and skin problems. Perhaps the most well-known effect of stress on our health is on our heart.

Our behaviour

Behaviour related to stress is often more difficult to identify – nail biting, excessive smoking and/or use of alcohol and other drugs are all signs. However, one of the most obvious signs is the intensification of our own personality traits.

Other symptoms may include feeling worried, irritated, demotivated or unable to cope and being less creative. We may also experience difficulty in concentration and in making decisions.

Our work

With all the above physical and behavioural symptoms, it is not surprising that our work is affected. Typically, the consequences are lower job satisfaction, communication breakdown and a focus on unproductive tasks.

All these symptoms may be experienced in normal life; they only become symptoms of stress when they do not have an obvious cause, when several of them come at the same time, or when we experience them more often than we would expect. Also, whilst the symptoms are often exhibited in our workplace behaviour, it should not be assumed that the symptoms are a reflection of workplace stressors. It is important to identify the source of stress and to differentiate between work factors and those in our lives generally.

Preventing stress

Recognising the symptoms and identifying the sources of stress are essential in developing the strategies necessary to help ourselves. Help may involve doing one of two things:

- removing or reducing outside pressures, or
- accepting the things that can't be changed.

The strategy may be as simple as accepting our weaknesses and restricting changes. Some very simple rules can create immediate effects:

- pace yourself, complete tasks rather than juggling 'too many balls in the air'
- take a break, don't be afraid to relax for a moment and regain your energy
- withdraw from the source of pressure, take a moment now and

then to step back and look at yourself and what you're doing
- communicate effectively, this can save time and energy
- forget the near misses
- look after your health
- take sensible exercise, it is a great way to relieve tension
- eat a sensibly balanced diet
- get enough sleep, waking refreshed to meet the demands of the day.

If these don't seem possible alone, then seek professional help! The most important rule is to accept ourselves as we are, to avoid blaming others or the environment and to take responsibility. It is possible to turn stress into a positive force.

Living with stress

Our lives are a minefield of pressures. These pressures come at us from different directions both at home and work; from others and from ourselves. To live successfully with such pressures, it is essential that we monitor ourselves and become aware of our personal signs.

Through such monitoring we should be able to identify what our triggers are and to manage our stress more effectively. There is a choice – stress doesn't have to run or ruin our lives. These simple steps will help:

- recognise our warning signs
- maintain perspective and balance
- take steps to reduce stress.

If we are suffering serious stress, change isn't an optional extra. Our happiness and well-being depend on making changes. When this comes, it will bring with it an easing of pressures, profound changes in personality and mood and an approach to life which benefits us and those with whom we live and work.

- If you have made a commitment to managing the stress in your life then the IM Publication *Successful Stress Management in a Week* by Cary L. Cooper and Alison Straw, will help. It is available from Lavis Marketing, 73 Lime Walk, Headington, Oxford, OX3 7AD Tel: 0345 023736 Fax: 01865 750079 for £5.99.

© *Institute of Management*

Wound-up over work

The results of the first Office Hours survey into secretarial stress are here. And the news isn't good. Emma Brockes reports.

Take a close look at your colleagues. If they are eating, emailing, or emitting a high-pitched whine in the manner of a mosquito, they are likely to be suffering from a condition that affects more than half of all office support workers. We all like to complain of stress – the classic ailment of the 21st-century office worker – from time to time, occasionally suffering minor meltdowns when everything gets just too much. Now a *Guardian* survey has provided the most concrete evidence yet of the affect of stress on secretarial and office support staff – and the news isn't good.

More than 15,000 of you responded to the Office Hours survey into workplace stress, and 52% said it was a major factor in your working life. The signs to watch out for include moaning to colleagues, compulsively snacking and indulging in personal use of the phone and email facilities. And the reason? Three main factors got most of the blame: quantity of work, difficult colleagues, and worries about a stress-filled future – beset with comfort-eating.

They are probably problems that most workers can relate to. But what was surprising was the violence of feeling you demonstrated about stress in the workplace. While three-quarters of respondents have never shouted at their boss, taken up smoking or displayed the external signs of nervous breakdown, the survey asked you to share what you would really, really like to tell your boss given the chance – and some fairly ferocious demons were unleashed. 'I'd tell her to shut up, stop being a hypocrite, stop getting on everyone's nerves,' runs a typically vitriolic response. 'Then I would punch her on the nose.'

One secretary dreamed of saying, 'Get stuffed you gutless little man', another aspired to castrating her boss. 'Go on a diet,' said another,

while one hard-done-by secretary – a particular favourite, this – wanted to yell: 'Do it yourself – and get a bath.' There is, presumably, some stress-busting value to these outbursts, but the vehemence with which they are expressed is a little alarming. There certainly seems to be some seething resentment bubbling under the businesslike air and polite telephone manner.

Fantasy scenarios aside, angry gripes seem to be based on three main legitimate grievances. Unrealistic expectations, particularly concerning deadlines, are perceived to be the most provocative of management abuses. 'I would ask him to communicate better so I could leave my crystal ball at home,' said one respondent, witheringly. 'I'd have him be me for a day so he can see how long things take, and that a five-minute deadline is not good enough,' said another, along with the sweet reminder, 'I'm important too'.

This sense of being under-appreciated was another common complaint, PAs sharing plaintive fantasies to 'tell him how I feel', hoping that the boss would 'involve me more and keep me informed', and 'say thank you'.

And, no surprise here, money is

the final source of upset, with respondents finding a variety of creative ways, some involving minor assault, to demand a pay rise. A lot of respondents appeared to have spent time formulating scenes in which they verbally incinerated their seniors. 'I'd ask him if he has to practise to be so obnoxious or whether it just comes naturally,' ran one insult that, one suspects, has been polished in front of the mirror in the ladies', but will never be used face to face.

Everybody needs to let off steam, and those of you who replied to the survey probably felt a lot better having shared your true feelings, on paper at least. But there is an important hidden reason for all this outrage. Just under half believed themselves to be stuck in the wrong job: fretting, resentful and storing up unhappiness to unleash at home. Apart from compulsively emailing and wailing to colleagues, the stressed majority found their condition expressing itself most seriously away from the office. A quarter of those who replied believed their sex life had deteriorated since starting their job; a third said stress was having a detrimental effect on their relationship with their partner. More than half had suffered from insomnia. And

yet, in spite of these hardships, almost two-thirds of respondents said they would be willing to take on more pressure for a salary increase.

More pressure is not, of course, the same thing as more stress, and respondents were keen to differentiate between an environment so hard-boiled it damaged them (such as harassment and bullying) and one in which they were merely given a daunting amount of responsibility. As stress becomes more prevalent, so sufferers learn to lessen its impact by fitting it into a sliding scale of harmfulness, a self-preservation mechanism common in workplaces where stress permeates the atmosphere as much as the air-conditioning. The majority of respondents recognised a difference between healthy and damaging stress, between that which stimulated the adrenalin and enabled them to meet deadlines, and that which caused mental paralysis.

Some industries are probably more difficult than others: 'There is still a culture in the legal profession that says if you aren't stressed, you're not working properly,' says Barry Pritchard of Solcare, the legal healthcare charity. 'We've had calls from people who were certain they'd lost their jobs because they had

'Employers treat stress very differently to other hazards. We have to stop them thinking that there are two kinds of hazard – one that they have to do something about and one that they can ignore'

complained about their workload.' But like a rather pernicious virus, stress can infect even the most seemingly cosy of work environments.

'There are quite a lot of companies that still think stress is a wimp's issue,' says Cary Cooper of the University of Manchester Institute of Science and Technology. 'This makes it particularly painful for male stress sufferers to seek help. If women are under a lot of pressure, they talk about it. That gives a release. Men are more likely to bottle it up, or turn to unhealthy coping mechanisms such as drinking.'

This is when stress becomes more than just something to be moaned about with your mates over

a bottle of wine. In a recent survey conducted by ICM, workplace tensions were found to have caused one in eight men and one in ten women to shout at colleagues. Many also admitted to having broken down in tears as a result of problems at work.

But the Office Hours survey found that while bosses were indirectly blamed for a stressful environment, the majority of respondents didn't think their jobs would be less stressful if they had a better relationship with their managers. It wasn't the stand-up fights and the tearful outbursts that caused stress, but the bitchy undercurrents that never made it to a confrontation and were thus never taken seriously.

This is the heart of the matter. 'Employers treat stress very differently to other hazards,' says Hugh Robertson, of the public services union Unison. 'We have to stop them thinking that there are two kinds of hazard – one that they have to do something about and one that they can ignore.' Employers: take note. Ignoring your stressed-out secretaries may be an occupational hazard. One day, they may decide to let you know how they really feel, and it won't be pretty.

Dealing with stress at work

Information from Mind in Manchester

What is stress?
Stress describes feelings we get when we have difficulty meeting all the physical and emotional demands life makes on us. At work it could be because a task is either too great or not challenging enough. A little stress can be useful in making us extra alert. Too much stress can affect our ability to do everyday things and can lead to headaches, insomnia, depression, anxiety, tiredness, irritability, overeating or drinking, over-sensitivity and lack of concentration.

What causes stress at work ?
MIND conducted a survey in 1992 of causes of stress. They were:

- pressure to perform and maintain quality
- recession and fear of redundancy
- change / pace of change
- increased workload due to reductions in staff
- excessive hours
- other personal problems, e.g. relationships, child care, finances also contribute towards stress.

What you can do about stress
Manage your time and your work:
- talk to your line manager. If they don't respond, talk to the personnel officer or your trade union representative.
- make sure your workload is not too big and your job description

realistic. Try to renegotiate it if it isn't.
- organise your work by drawing up realistic goals and time schedules.
- ask for regular supervision sessions with your manager to get feedback and air problems and ask for training if you need it.
- try not to take work home or do unpaid overtime.

Make your work environment right
- make it as comfortable as possible, with a suitable temperature and not too noisy.
- try to get adequate equipment to do your job.

- check if all health and safety standards are being met.
- you have a right to work free from harassment or discrimination.

Look after yourself
- take less caffeine in tea and coffee especially before sleep.
- get enough sleep and learn to relax. There are various relaxation techniques you can learn by joining a class or borrowing a tape or book from the library. Contact MIND for more information.
- take regular physical exercise for

20-30 minutes 2 or 3 times a week, for example walking, cycling, swimming, aerobics.
- eat healthily and sensibly, e.g. plenty of fibre, lots of fruit and vegetables, white meat and fish, less fatty and sugary foods.
- don't drink, smoke or take drugs to excess.
- consider holistic health options, e.g. acupuncture, homeopathy, herbalism, massage. They work for some people but are not available on the NHS and have to be paid for.

Talk to someone
- discuss your work situation with someone close, either connected with work or outside of it.
- check if there are any support groups where people with similar jobs share problems and support each other.
- check if your employer provides stress at work counselling. Some big employers do.

• The above information is from Mind in Manchester. See their web site at www.mind-in-manchester.org.uk

© *Mind in Manchester*

Our family life is being ruined say stressed bosses

By Laura Clark

The vast majority of Britain's bosses say their home lives are being ruined by stress at work, according to a report yesterday.

Three-quarters of executives reported that workplace pressure takes a damaging toll on their health, family relationships, sex drive and overall enjoyment of life.

Yet in today's 'macho' work culture, few admit to being unable to cope with stress levels, according to the study by the Institute of Management.

An alarming picture of executives buckling under increasing workloads, new technology and bullying by top management is painted by the research, which was undertaken jointly with health care firm PPP.

Bosses pinpointed a range of causes for pressures that can boil over into stress. These included meeting deadlines, constant interruptions, lack of support, incompetent superiors and poor internal communication.

Bullying is a further source of stress – one in ten say they regularly experience intimidation from those above.

Firms introducing new technology give managers the most stress, with almost seven in ten reporting heavier workloads in the past year.

Generally, 40 per cent struggle to meet goals, 42 per cent say they

are unable to cope with workloads, while 43 per cent are unhappy with workplace culture.

And the worryingly high 75 per cent report that stress has a serious effect on their home lives, according to the study of 819 managers, entitled *Taking the Strain*.

Most say they experience a number of symptoms as a result of workplace stress, including excessive tiredness and disturbed sleep. Seven in ten get bad tempered, 63 per cent suffer headaches and more than one in two report that their sex drive has dropped.

The most popular ways of coping are drinking, shopping, exercise and talking to family and friends.

Mary Chapman, director general of the Institute of Management, said: 'Leaders of organisations need to work with individuals and organisations to identify and deal with the root cause of stress, develop a healthier workplace culture and equip people with up-to-date skills.

'For individuals, it means learning to recognise and manage their own pressure points before they turn to stress.'

And Dudley S. Lusted, from PPP healthcare, said: 'Organisational

stress is essentially a risk management issue and as tools to address it are now to hand, employers who neglect it are clearly breaking the law, with potentially expensive consequences. Managers, too, must be brave in tackling organisational stress and do their part to challenge the misguided notion that taking excessive pressure without complaining is just part of the job.'

But David Hands, of the Federation of Small Businesses, said stress was 'part and parcel' of many managerial jobs and went hand in hand with increased responsibility.

'A lot of our members will suffer stress without laying too much emphasis on it,' he said. 'Some people even thrive on it.'

And Ruth Lea, head of policy at the Institute of Directors, said: 'People in high-flying jobs are going to get paid quite a lot of money. They are not being paid for collecting eggs. You have to be able to cope with the pressure.

'Frankly, if you can't or if the personal expense is too great, then get a less pressured job with less money.

'You can't have everything in this life and we have to make hard choices.'

© *The Daily Mail*
February, 2000

A problem shared . . .

Workplace stress is on the increase, but companies are now recognising the benefits of providing counselling for employees

We have all heard of the listening bank, but how about the listening boss? If that sounds too good to be true, you may have experienced a manager who dismisses his employees' emotional difficulties as none of his concern.

But as workplace stress continues to be a major reason for absenteeism, and the bill to the employer creeps upwards (the CBI put the cost of lost work days at £10bn in 1998), many companies are finally recognising the benefits of providing emotional support to their workers. And whether they opt for an in-house counselling service, or (more commonly) contract external counsellors, the message to anxious, depressed or stressed-out staff is that it's good to talk.

'Employee assistance programmes' – set up to help staff deal with any problem that may affect them at work – are becoming increasingly common. The Employee Assistance Professional Association estimates that more than 1,000 companies now offer workplace counselling services, reaching 700,000 employees.

Initial advice on issues such as legal queries, relationships, family issues and, of course, workplace problems is often available through a helpline service, which the employee can take further to a series of face-to-face counselling sessions.

'This kind of activity has been on the increase for the past ten years and increasingly so in the past five,' says Robert Westlake, chartered psychologist and managing director of the Personal Effectiveness Centre. 'The idea of people being more capable of talking and counselling is now more acceptable, and in bigger companies in particular people do feel they can own up to emotional problems. After all, if people have a health problem they

By Wendy Smith

take an aspirin – if they have an emotional problem, they see a counsellor.'

Troubles at home, coupled with the drive towards a leaner workforce and longer working hours, exacerbate stress and absenteeism. But while workplace worries affect everyone, it is often the secretary who is the most put upon, according to Dr Angela Hetherington, clinical director of workplace counsellors PPC. 'A manager may be particularly stressed and this anger is more likely to be directed down the line rather than up, and that next in line can often be the PA.'

Office rage, where managers become verbally abusive, is also on the increase, says Hetherington. 'The manager may tell the PA that she is no good at her job, doesn't dress the part, can't answer the phone properly – and the PA accepts that there is little she can do and that is why she comes for counselling.'

Other problems frequently raised in the privacy of the counsellors' rooms are work overload,

shifting responsibilities and the effects and speed of change. 'Research has shown that one of the causes of stress is lack of control of your workload,' says Westlake.

Some of us need a little pressure and stress to work effectively, but what are the symptoms of a person suffering from overload? 'The time to take note is when your performance starts to drop off,' according to Westlake. 'You forget things, have small accidents, inaccuracies appear in your work. Your boss may point it out and you feel overly aggrieved. You may not want to get up in the morning and you take more time off. It really is when the pressure overcomes your ability to work.'

Ernst & Young, which has 7,000 employees across the UK, introduced an employee assistance programme in October last year. A 24-hour telephone counselling and advice service is available to all staff. 'It is usually the first port of call,' explains Richard Gartside, Ernst & Young employee manager. 'If they need more help, they can have up to six face-to-face counselling sessions.' The service has not gone unnoticed – 7% of Ernst & Young staff phoned in after the launch. And while the counselling is confidential, recurrent generic workplace problems can be fed back to management and adjustments and action can be taken.

'Workplace counselling offers benefits to everyone,' says Hetherington. 'The employees get heard and help themselves in the short term, and we collate the information in a report back to the company which in turn helps other colleagues and the organisation in the long run.'

Much management emphasis in recent years has gone into being 'the organisation that learns'. Now it could be a case of support staff seeking out the organisation that listens.

Take it easy, it's only a job

One in five of us suffers measurable stress at work, says Liz Bestic, and employers are finally waking up to this . . .

Stressed? If you're an employee, you probably are. And if you're an employer, you definitely should be. A court ruling earlier this month awarded a council housing officer, Beverley Lancaster, £67,000 for workplace stress. Now Unison, the public sector union which represented her, has other cases in the pipeline. Statistics from Bristol University show that at least one in five of us now suffers from measurable stress at work, caused by long hours and lack of support.

New legislation places a 'duty of care' on companies to protect their workers from health and safety hazards, and that includes stress. Growing numbers of well-established companies have now adopted a holistic approach to their employees' well-being. At Unipart International, an automotive parts and accessories company based in Cowley, Oxford, there is a 'health and well-being centre' where employees can benefit from a range of alternative therapies including reflexology and aromatherapy. Absenteeism is low.

Barry Conway, 41, an Internet training and development manager, does not seem the type to waft about on an aromatherapy cloud. But thanks to his twice-weekly sessions, he now no longer gets the headaches that used to trouble him. 'I discovered aromatherapy two years ago and I'm evangelical about it now,' he says.

Barry now keeps a range of oils in his desk drawer and decides on which ones to burn for maximum results. 'Basil and lemon are the best ones to help stimulate concentration,' he says with authority.

Stress costs British industry £20bn a year, so it is in a company's financial interests to ensure that its workers are stress-free. At British Petroleum's offshore oil rigs, workers get massage treatments as part of a company drive to de-stress the workforce. Sue McGovern is an on-site masseuse. She visits the rigs once a month to treat the workers for bad backs, sleeplessness and general stress. 'An oil rig is one of the most stressful environments in which to work. The guys all have the shadow of Piper Alpha hanging over them, regular alarm drills when they have to abandon ship and a total lack of private space. Often they sleep three to a room and there is nowhere to escape, go for a walk or just be alone,' she says.

'Sixteen-hour shifts mean many of them work indoors with no natural light, and the ones that do work outside have to put up with the wind and rain and freezing conditions.'

Sue's treatments are so popular that she is booked up months ahead. 'A lot of these guys are really stressed out, but the feedback I get is very positive. Their sleep improves and their stress levels are down,' she says. 'There's no doubt it boosts people's morale to know that the company cares about them and values them.'

St Luke's advertising agency in central London has adopted an imaginative approach to keeping staff happy. Not only has it done away with the hierarchy of boss and worker, it also had a 'chill-out' room years before any other business did. 'The irony is that we no longer need the room because we have so many other things going on here, from on-site massage to yoga,' says the business manager, Juliet Soskice. 'Staff can either have a therapy at the Hale Clinic or six weeks' free membership of a local gym.

'St Luke's is a holistic environment as well as a workspace. The emotional well-being and physical health of staff is as important as how they perform in their job. It's a very simple equation; happier people equals better productivity.'

'That's all very well,' sniffs Cary Cooper, professor of organisational psychology at the University of Manchester's Institute of Science and Technology, 'but if you have an autocratic management style or a culture of long working hours, no amount of aromatherapy is going to do any good.

'It is up to the workforce and the employer together to recognise that overloading people and damaging their private lives is not the best way to manage human beings.

'Employers are too inflexible and need to wake up to the fact that in two out of every three families in the UK, both partners are working. That requires not longer hours but flexibility to allow them to work partly from home and partly from a central office,' he says.

'The culture of longer working hours and insecurity has made work very stressful. New technology was supposed to be our support system, but all it has done is speed up the pace and overload us with intolerable amounts of information.'

Off sick with stress

It causes a bigger loss of working time than colds. By Kate Hurry

Stress has overtaken the common cold as the biggest cause of sick leave from work, a survey has found.

One in three employers are providing stress counselling for staff amid growing concern about the impact on business.

And one in five companies with over 1,000 staff regard stress as a 'major problem'.

Yesterday health experts said they were not surprised at the findings.

Dr Rajinder Saggu, a Harley Street GP who specialises in treating people suffering stress at work, said billions of pounds were wasted each year because of man hours lost to stress-related illness.

'As a GP I tend to see people further down the line with alcohol or drug problems and people having nervous breakdowns,' he said.

Dr Saggu claimed that, despite the losses to business, many bosses were not interested in dealing with the problem. 'They do not see any direct financial gain in reducing stress,' he said.

He believes staff are becoming more susceptible to stress because of the increasing pace of work. New technology was partly responsible, he said, with faster responses and results expected.

He also believed the breakdown of the traditional family means work problems can become overwhelming.

'People are becoming more isolated as individuals,' he said. 'The extended family is going. People have not got as much support at home, which adds to stress.'

In addition, employees were working more hours, which perpetuated the cycle, he said. 'Although the law says we are supposed to work 48-hour weeks, employees who work more are scared to say anything for fear of reprisals.'

Last year, lost working days cost business £300million, with stress the biggest factor, according to figures from the Trades Union Congress. The survey, published by business information group Gee Publishing, found the problem was not entirely being ignored.

More managers are being trained to recognise and reduce stress at work, it said.

Some companies are even issuing employees with booklets on how to cope with stress.

Sally Harper, human resources manager at Gee Publishing, said: 'Growing evidence of the impact of stress on absence levels, coupled with recent legal awards against companies seems to have made this problem too big to ignore.'

The CBI, however, said that while stress was a key factor in lost work days, it was impossible to estimate the exact impact.

'It's difficult to quantify because people do not ring their offices and say: "I am having a day off because I am stressed",' a spokesman said. He added: 'It's important to remember that some level of stress is important for people's performance. You do not want to be falling asleep at your desk.

'There are things companies can do, in particular ensuring staff have the right support, resources and training to do their work.'

© The Daily Mail,
April, 2000

Half of workers suffer stress

By Gary Finn

One British worker in five is left feeling worthless by the job while almost half lose sleep because they are worrying about work, a survey has found. In one of the widest studies into stress in the workplace, researchers at Warwick University analysed 7,500 workers in 16 European countries to assess how changing work patterns over the past five years had affected their lives.

British workers emerged as some of the most stressed in Europe behind employees in the former East Germany, Greece and Italy. Belgian workers were the least stressed, followed by the Spanish and Portuguese.

The research was carried out by Warwick's Professor of Economics, Andrew Oswald, and fellow economist Professor David Blanchflower at Dartmouth College, New Hampshire, in the United States.

More than half the European workers surveyed found that stress levels and responsibility had increased and there was evidence of strain, lost sleep and depression. Half of British workers reported more pressure than five years ago compared with only 40 per cent of Belgians. The survey also highlighted a growing sense of alienation. At least one worker in five admitted feeling 'a worthless person' at work and up to one-third lost confidence in themselves.

Professor Oswald said: 'I think there is some reason for concern here . . . when working life for the bulk of European employees has got much more pressurised in just five years and it has become easier for almost none, I do worry about exactly what is going on out there.'

The Trades Union Congress welcomed the research and said last night it should 'ring alarm bells' with employers. A spokesman said: 'It is an increasing phenomenon of the modern workplace but sadly an unsurprising element of this study is the feeling of worthlessness workers are experiencing.' He said British industry lost about £5bn a year through people being off work from stress-related illness.

© The Independent
April, 2000

Absence cost business £10 billion in 1999 – says survey

Information from the Confederation of British Industry

Workplace absence cost British business £10.5 billion in 1999, an average of £438 per worker.

This is the main finding of an annual survey, released today (Thursday), by the Confederation of British Industry and PPP healthcare. The survey shows that costs have risen slightly when compared to the previous year. In 1998, the total cost was £10.2 billion, an average of £426 per worker.

Employees take off an average of 7.8 days per year, a fall from last year when 8.5 days were lost per employee. This suggests that 187 million working days were lost in 1999, 3.4 per cent of working time.

Manual employees took off more time than non-manual employees, but absence among both groups declined. Among non-manual employees absence fell to 6.5 days from 7.6 days in the previous year. Absence among manual employees fell to 9.2 days from 9.4 days.

Small firms had lower absence rates than large firms. Around nine days were lost per employee among companies employing over 500 employees, which compares to just 4.8 days among companies employing less than 50 employees.

Private sector employees took, on average, 2.8 days fewer than their public sector counterparts. Public sector absence was 9.9 days per employee in 1999, compared to 7.1 days per employee in the private sector.

John Cridland, CBI's Human Resources Policy Director, said: 'Absence is a huge cost to business and the worst performing firms have twice the absence rates of the best ones. Most absence is caused by genuine minor illness, but it is important for firms to ensure unnecessary absence is reduced – benchmarking performance against similar firms will reveal problem areas. One clear message from the survey is that absence needs to be actively managed at a senior level. It is only by understanding the causes of absence that managers can design the right policies to tackle this important issue.'

The survey shows that many companies have reduced the amount of time employees take off by giving senior or HR managers responsibility for managing absence, rather than line managers.

Employers said that return to work interviews are the best policy for managing absence. Other successful practices include discipline procedures, formal notification procedures and occupational health services.

Dudley Lusted, PPP healthcare's director of corporate healthcare development, said: 'It is clear that absence management needs to be more sophisticated. Long-term absence and stress-related problems are ranked worryingly high as causes of absence. While return to work interviews and other practices are effective management tools for short-term absences, managing these other causes of absence requires, among other things, early access to professional medical and psychological support. Companies that fail to recognise this and manage the underlying issues of absence will never reach the 5.3 days' absence levels achieved by the best-performing companies.'

The regions with the highest absence rates for manual employees were in the Southern region (12 days), the North West (12 days) and the Eastern and Welsh regions (11 days). Regions with the lowest rates were the South East, Northern and Scottish regions.

For non-manual employees the highest absence rates were in the Eastern and Southern regions (9 days) and Yorkshire and Humber (8 days). Scotland, Wales and the Northern region recorded the lowest absence levels for non-manual employees.

© Confederation of British Industry (CBI)

Rising stress brings 'desk rage' at work

By Seumas Milne, Labour Editor

Workplace stress and long hours are creating a growing phenomenon of desk rage, with more employees having arguments and breaking down under pressure, according to a survey published today.

Workers are being driven to drink, insomnia, and illness by overwork, tougher targets and deadlines, and rudeness from clients and colleagues, according to ICM Research in the latest survey to highlight stress at work. As a result, workers are turning on each other.

Nearly two-thirds of 600 employees who were questioned said that they suffered from workplace stress, which another survey last month found to be worse in Britain than anywhere else in Europe or North America, and more than half said they had lost sleep because of anxiety.

Some 43% said they had had to work 12-hour days or more to satisfy their bosses, with 60% blaming a growing workload for their stress, 40% citing the pressure of targets, and 38% deadlines. One in five said that problems with colleagues were triggering desk rage.

Both government and business face increasing demands to act over stress, insecurity, and long hours at work. In July, Birmingham city council paid a record £67,000 to a former housing officer in compensation for work-related stress, and around 500 other cases are before the courts.

Meanwhile, the government will come under attack at this month's TUC conference in Brighton for attempting to water down the impact of European working hours protection for white-collar workers and professionals, the group seen as having suffered the sharpest increase in work insecurity and stress.

> **'We are now seeing desk rage, as stress builds to intolerable levels and conflicts boil over between colleagues'**

ICM's survey found workplace stress had led 29% of workers to have a row with a colleague, while 28% had drunk too much and one in four had fallen ill as a result of work tension and pressure.

A third said that they had been forced to miss a social engagement because of work, and only 17% were always able to take a lunchbreak, with more than one in five blaming their office culture for missed lunch hours.

The proportion saying they were sometimes unable to take a meal break reached 92% in the Midlands.

One in three reached for cigarettes under stress, while 30% of women and 15% of men said they turned to chocolate.

Workplace tensions had caused 16% of men and 9% of women to shout at colleagues, the survey found, while 6% of women and 1% of men admitted having broken down in tears as a result of problems at work.

Commenting on the findings, Sue Keane of the British Psychological Society said that they showed that the 'lunch is for wimps' culture of the 1980s was still alive.

'We are now seeing desk rage, as stress builds to intolerable levels and conflicts boil over between colleagues,' she said.

'Just a few minutes out of the office or workplace at lunchtime could make all the difference.'

© Guardian Newspapers Limited, 2000

Learning to cope with stress

Information from MIND

There are a number of things you can do on your own to help manage stress. They include:

- managing your time more effectively.
- enjoying more relaxing sleep.
- breathing exercises to encourage relaxation.
- relaxing properly.
- taking a little extra physical exercise.
- eating a healthy diet.

Four ways to manage your time more effectively

Here are four simple pointers:

- make a list of the things you have to do in any given day. These are your priorities, everything else can be left until later.
- of your priorities, make a list in descending order of importance. This means that the really important tasks come first.
- stick to your list. Take each task one at a time and don't start the next one until the previous one is finished. If you try to do too many at once you'll end up muddled and possibly accomplish little.
- at the end of each day sit back and reflect on what you have done and what you have achieved, rather than spending your time worrying about what still needs to be done.

Achieving more relaxing sleep

As many as one in five people suffer insomnia – often this is due to stress. Here are some simple measures to help you establish a better sleeping pattern:

- create the right environment for you to sleep. Use earplugs if it is too noisy, thicker curtains if street light disturbs you.
- wake at the same time each day. You will find you gradually feel sleepy at the same time each night.

- wind down in readiness for sleep by following a daily routine: a short walk, listen to the radio, have a warm bath.
- do relaxation and breathing exercises (more information is available from Mind).

Breathing properly

How you breathe has a major impact on how how feel. There are special breathing exercises we can help you with if you have difficulty in this area. Just send for our specialist booklet *Mind Guide to Managing Stress* (cost £1.00 plus 31 pence postage and packing) for detailed information. Essentially, though, you should take time each day to sit or lie down, relax and, for a few minutes, breathe deeply so that your abdomen moves up and down but your upper chest does not.

Simple relaxation

Relaxation is the natural antidote to stress. Everyone should take time at intervals in the day, perhaps between important tasks, to relax. Here is a simple relaxation routine which only takes a few minutes:

- sit upright if possible in a comfortable chair. Have a good stretch then let your shoulders and arms relax and close your eyes. Ease off the tension in your scalp, forehead, jaws and neck. Relax your chest, your arms, your lower back, your thighs and knees. Feel the tension easing in your knees, your calves and, finally, feet and toes.
- breathe using the breathing techniques already described.
- imagine a special place which would be especially peaceful to you – or remember one from your past and, for a few moments, imagine you are there.

A little regular exercise

Exercise uses up the adrenalin and other hormones which we produce naturally under stress as the body and mind prepare for fight or flight. Exercise doesn't have to be strenuous or competitive. Walking at a reasonably fast pace for 20 minutes a day is said to be one of the best forms of exercise you can take.

Hobbies, interests and a healthy diet

Hobbies and pastimes which take your mind off daily worries also contribute to reducing stress, while a diet rich in carbohydrates and fibre and low in fat, sugar and salt gives your body and brain the right balance of nutrition for a greater sense of well-being.

Want to know more about stress and how to cope?

If you would like more detailed information on stress, please send for our booklet: *The Mind Guide to Stress* (cost £1.00 plus 31 pence postage and packing) which also contains many useful references for further reading. © *MIND*

Flora facts – stress

Information from the Flora Project for Heart Disease Prevention

What is stress?

In a dark underpass, a shadowy figure appears, blocking your exit. Could it be a mugger? . . .

Automatically your body switches to 'red alert'. You feel fear. . . Your senses sharpen. Hormones flood into your bloodstream, causing you to breathe more deeply and making your heart rate soar. Your muscles tense in anticipation.

You are ready for action – be it to tackle this potential aggressor or turn and run like mad!

Your body was in tune with the threat you sensed and instinctive reactions primed you for self-survival.

This is an extreme case, but some stress is part of everyday life. In fact, it is essential – it helps keep us on our toes and out of danger, after all, we need to be alert when crossing a busy road.

Unfortunately there are times when we feel we can no longer cope with our stress and it becomes DISTRESS. It is as if we develop a 'hair trigger' and become tense in everyday situations such as traffic jams, or even when the morning paper is five minutes late. Even simple things make us 'blow a fuse'.

Frequent surges of stress hormones prime our bodies to run from things we can never escape.

After all, no matter how tightly you grip the steering wheel, you will be stuck in the rush hour jam. These pent-up feelings can push up blood pressure and put a strain on the whole body including the heart.

If you think you are a stress sufferer, DON'T PANIC! Medical problems are not inevitable and there are many ways you can get your stress responses back in tune.

Who is prone to stress?

If you answered 'yes' to some of our questions, 'The tell-tale signs of stress', there's a good chance that your stress level is a bit high. You are probably hard working, have a lot of drive and enjoy a challenge. The sort of personality that some doctors call 'Type A'. They call the other side of the personality coin 'Type B'. These people have an easy-going manner, they are relaxed, calm and won't make a drama out of crisis. Like all attempts to categorise, splitting people into two types is a bit unrealistic – we all exhibit a mixture of both behaviours. The key thing is to try and modify your behaviour so that it becomes more B and less A – basically trying to take a more relaxed attitude to life and its problems.

A good way to start is to list all the things that cause you stress. Is it

the train that's late (again!); the neighbour's dog that barks; the person that lights up in the no smoker; the complicated wedding arrangements; the queue or the traffic jam; the rude receptionist; the search for a new home?

Make a list and learn to recognise your stress triggers. Once you have identified your 'triggers' consciously try to relax in these situations, and learn to tackle the source of the problem, where possible.

What can I do to avoid stress?

1. Remember your 'stress situations' and when you get caught up in one, use it as a cue to relax. When the traffic is making you 'tense up', do the opposite. Give your arms and neck a stretch – try smiling at someone else caught in the jam.

2. When the phone is engaged, or the taxi ignores you, take a deep breath and exhale slowly – think how silly it seems that minor hassles like these made you uptight.

3. How much exercise do you get? Gentle rhythmic cycling, jogging or swimming are ideal ways of reducing the tension caused by stress. They help release all that

pent-up energy and will encourage deep refreshing sleep. Yoga, body conditioning classes or relaxation techniques may also be helpful.

4. Try to cut down on drinking and smoking. If you use these to 'unwind', the relief can only be temporary. They will not solve the problems that make you tense.

5. Stop trying to do more than one thing at a time. Take jobs in order of importance and try to plan ahead. Take control and have a positive action plan. You'll soon find that instead of doing everything at the last minute, you can get things done at a relaxed pace.

6. Instead of talking at other people, try having conversations with them and listen to what they say. Over lunch, eat more slowly, savour your food, forget work problems and have a good look round.

The tell-tale signs of stress

- Do you feel guilty when relaxing – uneasy if not 'on the go'?
- Do you lie awake worrying about tomorrow?
- Are you tense . . . does your neck feel 'knotted up'?
- Are you impatient or irritable – do you interrupt when others are talking?
- Are you smoking or drinking more – do you eat in a hurry?
- Does life seem full of crises – are you always having rows?
- Do you find it difficult to make decisions?
- Do you feel frustrated when people don't do what you want?
- Do you frequently experience a butterfly stomach, a dry mouth, sweaty palms or a thumping heart?

If you have said yes to some of these, read on . . .

Risk factors – the big 6

Remember that stress is one of the several factors causing heart disease – there are five others to bear in mind.

Help your heart by making healthier food choices

Excess weight puts a strain on your heart

Avoid a high blood pressure

Relax and reduce your stress levels

Take regular exercise

You should try to give up smoking

• For more information contact The Flora Project for Heart Disease Prevention, 24-28 Bloomsbury Way, London WC1A 2PX. Tel: 0800 446464, or either of the organisations listed below.
Coronary Prevention Group, 42 Store Street, London WC1E 7DB. British Heart Foundation, 14 Fitzhardinge Street, London W1H 4DH.

Stress and anxiety

Information from the Mental Health Foundation

Dealing with stress and anxiety

The first important step in tackling stress or anxiety is realising that it is causing you a problem. It is necessary to make the connection between feeling tired or ill and the pressures you are faced with. Do not ignore physical warnings such as tense muscles, over-tiredness, headaches or migraines.

The second step is to review your lifestyle. Are you taking on too much? Are there things you are doing which could be handed over to someone else? Can you do things in a more leisurely way? You may need to prioritise things you are trying to achieve and reorganise your life so that you are not trying to do everything at once.

Some problems may be more complicated and need to be dealt with head-on. If you are going through a bad patch in your marriage, for instance, you have to begin to talk things through. This might be difficult to do unaided, so you may need to call on outside help. There are a number of organisations which can help you in this way such as Relate which can provide someone to act as a 'referee'.

You must also make time for relaxation. Saying 'I just can't take the time off' is of little use if you are forced to take time off later through illhealth. Striking a balance between responsibility to others and responsibility to yourself is vital to reducing levels of stress in your life. Relaxation training can help you learn about techniques such as control of muscular tension and correct breathing. Alternatively you could try to allocate more time for leisure activities such as sports, hobbies or evening classes.

If possible, try to keep smoking and drinking to a minimum. They may seem to reduce tension, but in fact they can make problems worse. They can put you at more risk of physical consequences of stress because of the damage done to the body. You may also find it helpful to reduce the amount of coffee you are drinking as the effects of caffeine on the body can be very similar to the effects of stress and anxiety.

Seeking help

Do not be afraid to seek professional help if you feel that you are no longer able to manage things on your own. Many people feel reluctant to seek help as they feel that it is an admission of failure. This is not the case and it is important to get the help you need at the right time so that you can begin to get better.

The first person to approach is your family doctor. He or she should be able to advise about treatment and may refer you to another local professional such as a counsellor or psychiatrist. Treatment can involve talking your problems through with someone trained to deal with stress conditions and may also mean the use of medication for a short period. There are also a number of voluntary organisations which can provide help, both with tackling the causes of stress and with advising about ways of getting better.

Women and stress

Information from the Threshold Women and Mental Health Initiative

All human activity involves stress – in its widest sense, it arises any time there is an interaction between an individual and the outside world. We experience stress not only when we are anxious, furious or miserable but also when something exciting, desirable or gratifying happens. And although we tend to think that it is caused by excessive tension, it is more accurate to describe stress as generated by our response to an inappropriate level of pressure.

When we get the balance right, we experience the kind of energy and dynamism that makes stress not only an essential but also a positive experience. It is only when there is an imbalance between the demands we experience and our capacity to fulfil them that stress is felt to be a negative factor in our lives.

Many women face stressful situations – such as poverty, isolation, the 'double shift' – which it is hard to do much about. Interestingly, it has been shown that there is a strong link between stress/heart disease and low status or monotonous jobs – particularly where there are high demands coupled with minimal reward or satisfaction. Social isolation is another factor linked with stress-related illnesses, and here it is worth remembering that 95% of single parents are women. Thus the very conditions that characterise the traditionally female roles of child rearing, housework and caring for dependants mean that women may be highly vulnerable to stress-linked disorders.

As women, moreover, we often tend to put our own requirements aside – to put others first. We may neglect our own needs for relaxation and renewal in our lives, or forget that we have a responsibility for our own well-being too.

What is stress?

Our systems have a store of adaptive energy that is released the moment we are faced with a stressful situation. A chain of automatic physical responses is rapidly activated – often known as fight or flight reactions – causing our heart rate and respiration to increase, and our blood pressure to rise. Our digestive system closes down, the liver produces more glucose for fuel, our pupils dilate, our muscles tense ready for action, and our skin sweats in preparation for vigorous activity.

These responses of instantaneous and drastic bodily activity date from the period in our evolution when our survival depended on a rapid physical response to danger. In today's world however, it is often impossible – or inappropriate – to express this surge of energy by direct action. We may be unable to confront or run away from our 'stressors', – or we may immediately encounter another stressor, which leaves our bodies with no chance to return to a more normal state. This can cause our physical and emotional functions to become unbalanced.

It is ironic that the very physiological changes that were designed to get us out of trouble can now become dangerous themselves. For example, a permanently increased

heart rate can lead to chronic high blood pressure, and frequent surges of adrenalin into the bloodstream can increase the risk of clotting.

How to recognise stress

When we are under pressure our whole body responds, and any part of our system can show a reaction.

- On the physical level we may experience breathlessness, a pounding heart, trembling, a tense back, insomnia or digestive disturbances. Other common signs that our bodies are struggling with stress are headaches, a dry mouth, muscle and joint disorders and a weakened immune system. Eventually, our reserves of adaptive energy may become exhausted, leading to burnout.
- The mental symptoms can range from forgetfulness, difficulty in concentrating or in making decisions, to feeling unable to cope, or becoming suddenly panicky in specific situations.
- Our behaviour may change: we may feel restless, tired all the time, lose our appetite or overeat, neglect our personal appearance, or overindulge in alcohol, tobacco or other drugs.
- Emotionally, stress can make us feel tearful, paranoid, irritable, depressed or apathetic, and our self-confidence may evaporate.

Many of us just develop problems in one or two areas – our own particular weak spots. However, it is important to remember that some of these symptoms can cause permanent damage – that may in turn lead to such life-threatening conditions as asthma, stomach ulcers, coronary heart disease and even some forms of cancer. Developing awareness of our own vulnerable areas is important in order that we protect ourselves from stress-induced diseases.

Self-help for stress

There are three main strategies for dealing with undue stress in our lives.

1. Eliminate stressful situations.
Obviously there will always be some difficulties over which we have no control. However, it is worth examining recurring 'hot spots' with a view to defusing distressing situations. For instance, we can stop ourselves from overworking by learning to delegate – and to ask for help. Or, by taking time out to evaluate our regular commitments, we can learn to become better organised. Whether it is by eliminating unnecessary work, or simply by making lists, this act of prioritising can lead to a more manageable – and therefore appropriate – workload.

2. Learn to cope better with stressful situations.
On a physical level, becoming aware of our body's way of reacting to stress is the first step. We may for example notice a tightening of the neck muscles, or a churning stomach.

Learning a relaxation technique that connects body awareness with breathing can help to change these responses.

Yoga and meditation, practised regularly, can also be very helpful in reducing not only physical but also mental tension.

On an emotional level, it is worth looking at the ways we experience our frustration, anger and fear. When our perceptions and beliefs about the world cause us excessive stress, it may be time to readjust them. Perhaps we expect too much from others – perfectionists are very prone to stress.

Some women find it impossible to say 'no' without experiencing guilt, and may find assertiveness training helpful, as the low self-esteem felt by many of us makes it hard to express our negative feelings appropriately. Finding new and more fruitful ways of dealing with stressful situations can be very liberating – and is often easier in the company of other women.

3. Seek out activities that reduce the experience of stress.
Competitive physical sports such as squash or tennis are a good way of letting go of the aggression created by unresolved stressful situations.

Jogging, dancing, cycling, swimming, aerobic exercise and tai chi are also excellent methods of releasing pent-up tension via bodily exertion.

Laughter is another powerful de-stressor as it triggers off a surge of the feel-good hormone serotonin into the body. We can help to achieve this by making time to take part in activities that we enjoy. When we smile, the blood supply to the brain increases, feeding it with essential nutrients which create a positive mood.

Rest and diet: Getting enough sleep and maintaining a healthy eating habit are also ways that we can help restore our physical equilibrium, as are avoiding cigarettes, alcohol and other drugs.

Talking about problems with someone else nearly always helps. This could be with a friend, a family member, or a counsellor, or it could involve finding (or even starting) a self-help group.

Although we are programmed for fight or flight, it is nevertheless possible to modify our instinctive reactions – habitual responses to stress can be relearnt. Just as we can adapt in other ways, we can learn to replace unhelpful ways of responding with techniques that aim to reduce damage to our systems and to restore a more healthy balance to our minds and bodies.   © Threshold Women & Mental Health Initiative, 2000

Stress and your heart

Information from the Coronary Prevention Group

What causes stress?

Stress comes in all shapes and sizes. Any change in life's routine, pleasant or unpleasant, can cause stress. Divorce, the death of a partner, having an accident or an illness, retiring, getting married or pregnant, going on holiday, changing jobs… all these things can be stressful. Tension and conflict, and even niggling things like family rows or loss of sleep can cause stress if they're allowed to build up.

Some people suffer long-term stress, for example from the threat of redundancy, or constant family problems, from loneliness or depression, or from ill health – either their own or someone else's. Looking after young children at home can be very stressful too.

The environment can be a cause of stress: noise levels, pollution, over-crowding, bad working conditions or bad housing.

It's important to remember though that it's not always the *situation* that makes you feel stressed. Very often it is the *way you react* to it. For example, some people get very tense and angry if they get stuck in a traffic jam, while others take it quite calmly. And what is stressful to one person may be stimulating to another. Pressure at work might be worrying for one person whereas someone else would see it as a challenge.

The amount of *control* we have over stressful situations is important here. The more control we have over our lives, the less likely we are to feel stressed.

How your body reacts to stress

The way we react to stress has changed since the days when our ancestors had to fight for survival.

When you're under stress your body produces the powerful hormone adrenalin which gears you up for immediate action – what is sometimes called the 'fight or flight' response. This hormone gives you the extra energy either to face up to the challenge or to beat a hasty retreat.

You might have already noticed the outward signs of stress, perhaps before a job interview, or giving a speech at a wedding, or even when you're having a row with someone: a pounding heart, short, fast breathing, a dry mouth and clammy hands. Your heart fells as if it is pounding because it is working extra hard to pump blood to the parts of your body where it is needed most: the muscles and the brain. You breathe faster in order to get more oxygen. Priority is given to what's urgent, so blood is re-routed from tasks like digestion which can wait. The dry mouth is the body's way of telling you not to let any more food enter the digestive system. And the clammy hands are a sign that your body is sweating more to cool you down during the exertion.

The body reacts to stress in other, less noticeable ways too. As blood is rapidly pumped around the body, your blood pressure rises. Your blood becomes stickier and better able to clot, so that any wounds can be healed more easily. And the liver releases sugar and fats into your bloodstream to give you instant energy. The whole body is now ready for action. This fight or flight reaction which served our ancestors well, is less useful today. Modern problems can be difficult to fight and perhaps impossible to run away from, for example, living in bad housing, trouble at home or even getting stuck in a traffic jam.

Is stress bad for you?
A certain amount of stress can spur you on to get things done. Some people enjoy a certain amount of pressure in their lives but too much stress can have unwanted side effects and can be bad for you.

How can stress harm your heart?
To understand how stress can harm your heart, it helps to know something about how the heart works.

The coronary arteries are the most important blood vessels in the body, providing the heart with a rich and continuous supply of oxygen. The heart cannot do its job unless it gets enough oxygen.

A heart attack happens when a blood clot gets stuck in a furred-up artery and stops the flow of blood to the heart muscle. The result is pain, damage to the heart and sometimes death.

So how can stress affect the heart? The high blood pressure caused by stress can mean more wear and tear on the heart, and the stickiness of blood increases the risk of blood clots forming. If the extra supplies of sugars and fats released from the liver are not used up in energy, then they're available to form more atheroma, causing the arteries to fur up even more.

The link between stress and coronary heart disease is difficult to prove scientifically, partly because it is so difficult to define stress. Research does show, however, that people who are under more stress are more likely to get coronary heart disease and that alleviating stress may reduce the risk of a heart attack.

Stress and other factors
There is already good evidence that you are more likely to get coronary heart disease if:
- you smoke;
- you have a high blood cholesterol level;
- you have raised blood pressure.

Raised blood pressure and high levels of cholesterol in the blood are affected by your diet and by the amount of exercise you take. If you also suffer from stress, then you may have an even greater risk of getting coronary heart disease.

And you could find yourself in a vicious circle. If your way of coping with stress is to smoke or drink more or to eat more fatty foods, this could put you at greater risk.

Some of the things you may do to cope with stress are themselves risk factors for coronary heart disease.

© Coronary Prevention group

One-minute stress beaters

Self therapy

Too much stress is bad for your health, but the problem is that many pressure-management techniques can leave you feeling even more tense than before.

That's because they can take weeks to master and then need to be practised for 15 to 30 minutes a day in order to produce any lasting effect.

Dr David Lewis, a leading international expert on stress management, has devised a series of fast and effective techniques for controlling tension.

Not only are these easy to learn, but they take just 60 seconds to perform. That means you can start reducing your stress levels whenever you have a spare minute – perhaps when you're waiting at a traffic light, during a work break, or when you're about to go into a difficult meeting.

You can also use these 60-second stress-busters at the end of a hectic day and that way avoid taking work-related problems home.

Calm commuting
The daily commute to work on congested roads or crowded public transport can be highly stressful. And because travelling often involves sitting for long periods without adequate neck support, tension quickly develops in the muscles, leading to stiffness, headaches and increased bodily stress. Here are some ways to deal with commuting stress:

Inhale deeply while gently raising your shoulders in a shrug. Hold the tension for a moment, then exhale, lowering shoulders and allowing them to sag. As you breathe out, imagine the tension flowing out of your neck and shoulder muscles. Repeat three times.

Now spread and stretch fingers, breathing in deeply while doing so. Exhale and relax fingers. Repeat three times. Make fists, inhaling as you do so. Hold tension for a moment and then release, exhaling as you do. Repeat three times.

Turn head gently from side to side then nod. Do all this slowly, avoiding any abrupt motion which might cause strain. Repeat these exercises at regular intervals when travelling.

Apply a few drops of bergamot, melissa or peppermint essential oil to a handkerchief and inhale whenever you start feeling stressed. This clears the head and helps you feel more relaxed.

Daily worries

Major stress problems are often an accumulation of the trivial irritations, frustrations and setbacks that make up the everyday hassles of life. The following techniques will help you cope with daily problems.

- For instant relaxation, try 'hand-warming'. When we are stressed, blood is diverted away from the small vessels directly beneath the skin and sent deeper into the muscles in preparation for vigorous action. By consciously reversing this natural process, you can lower arousal and reduce stress.

  This is done by making one hand warmer than the other. There is nothing mystical or even especially difficult about this, although it does take practice.

  Start with your dominant hand (your right if right-handed), and imagine it becoming warmer. Just by concentrating on the idea of heat flowing into your fingers and palm, you may achieve a significant rise in temperature.

  Alternatively, place the palm of your dominant hand close to – but not touching – your cheek. Your cheek naturally radiates a good deal of heat. Feel this gently warming your hand.

  Keep breathing slowly and deeply; allow the feeling of warmth from your palm to spread down the arm and through your whole body, until you feel deeply relaxed. (You can test your 'before' and 'after' results with a liquid-crystal thermometer, which changes colour to indicate change in temperature.)
- Muscle relaxation will reduce physical and mental stress. First, you need to learn to tense the

major muscles individually (once you've mastered this technique, you'll see results in as little as 60 seconds). Sit or lie down in a quiet room. Start with the forearms, tensing them by bending the hands back.

When tensing any muscle in this exercise, hold the position to a count of five, then relax before moving on to the next muscle. (It's important not to hold your breath, but to breathe continuously and evenly, drawing the air deep into your lungs.)

Then move on to the biceps (try to touch the back of wrists to shoulders), triceps (stretch arms out as straight as possible), shoulders (shrug as hard as you can, press head back against chair or bed), forehead (frown and screw up eyes), mouth (clench jaw and force tongue against roof of mouth), chest (hold a deep breath, pull in stomach – this is the only time you hold your breath), legs (stretch, point toes, squeeze buttocks).

Now tense as many of the major muscle groups as possible at once, hold for a slow count to five, then flop.

Focus booster

To reduce concentration stress, warm hands by rubbing together. Then place over face, palms covering the eyes and fingers crossing on forehead. Don't press against eyeballs. Relax, shut your eyes.

After a few seconds stroke fingertips outwards from centre of your forehead. Repeat three times.

Place first two fingers of each hand on your temples and rub gently, using circular movements. After a few moments, move your fingers a little way up or down the temple, repeat.
- A great deal of avoidable stress arises from poor posture. Stand upright and lengthen entire spine so that it's straight. Keep buttocks taut and flatten stomach by pulling in abdominal muscles.

  Raise ribcage by lengthening your waist and let shoulders drop down and keep them relaxed. Raise your head so that chin is parallel with the ground (don't tilt head back). Imagine a pivot running through your ears – let your head fall forward on this pivot.

  Raise head, simultaneously pulling back shoulders and straightening spine. Practise regularly until this becomes your normal posture when standing and moving around.
- Arguments, unforeseen bad news or aggressive encounters can produce a sudden surge in stress.

The following techniques will help:
1. Find somewhere quiet and private. Loosen your tie and open the top buttons of your shirt or blouse. Sit or lie back.

Use the massage relaxation technique outlined previously to reduce physical stress, then perform the following face massage (if possible, use a massage oil containing lavender or neroli essential oil – half a teaspoon is usually enough for face and neck). With both hands (fingers together but using fingertips only), start under your chin.

Apply firm, gentle strokes, moving out towards your ears. Gently massage cheekbones, travelling up each side of nose to the forehead. Massage eyebrows then circle the eyes, moving up the nose and across the forehead as far as the hairline.

Repeat from the bridge of nose to forehead several times. Stroke down the nose, chin and throat in one continuous line; then gently stroke face and neck.

2. Many people get into the habit of holding their breath when they are stressed, but it's important to keep breathing slowly and deeply if you are to remain in control.

Sit or stand comfortably. Inhale, counting slowly and silently, up to six. Exhale, counting back from six to zero (don't hold your breath between each inhalation and exhala-tion). As you inhale, imagine a crystal-clear fluid entering your body and helping cleanse away all traces of stress.

As you exhale, imagine all the stress flowing out through your nostrils. Repeat five times.

Welcome relaxers
Bringing work stress home can lead to squabbles, fights, frustration, guilt – and even more stress. Prevent this by trying these techniques:
- Set aside some time for yourself soon after you get home. After one minute of deep muscle relaxation (see above), spend another 60 seconds calming your mind.

Despite its New Age associations, meditation is simply a technique for concentrating and calming the mind – and brief meditation can be mastered easily. Sit down, half-close your eyes and focus on a spot in the ground. You may find it helpful to place a coloured dot, about the size of a coin, on the floor or wall. Breathe slowly and deeply while concentrating on the spot.

For 60 seconds, try not to pay attention to anything but that spot. As your concentration falters, bring your mental focus gently back to the coloured dot. Stand up slowly and try to carry those feelings of relaxation through the rest of the day.
- Foot massage is an effective way of ensuring restful sleep. Sit down and place your right ankle over your left knee. Holding the right foot in one hand, rub the entire sole with the fingers of your other hand using firm pressure. Repeat with your left foot.

Getting off to a good start
Use these techniques to ensure a stress-free start to the day:
- Before getting out of bed prepare your system for the transition from sleep to action by gently stretching your muscles. Flex the toes of your right foot towards the shinbone, and inhale slowly and deeply. Hold breath for a moment then, while exhaling, curl your toes. Repeat three times.

Now repeat the exercise with your left foot. Finally, lengthen your body in a long, languid movement. Push downwards with each foot in turn to stretch your leg muscles. Stretch your arms one after the other above your head while exhaling. Slowly get out of bed and stand upright with your weight evenly balanced. Take two breaths. Curl toes inwards while inhaling and flex them while exhaling. Repeat this action three times.
- Give your system a bit of zest by putting a couple of drops of clary sage essential oil into warm – not hot – water and inhaling deeply while gently splashing the water onto your face.
- Take ginseng to boost your resistance to stress. Research has shown that this ancient Chinese tonic enhances our ability to resist stress as well as increasing alertness.
- Listening to the daily litany of disaster and death on the morning news can prove extremely stressful. It's far more sensible to lift your spirits by playing a favourite gentle piece of music.

- The above is an extract from *One-Minute Stress Management* by Dr David Lewis, published by Vermilion.

© Vermilion

Eating your stress away . . .

More than 30 million working days every year are lost because employees are suffering from stress. And according to a recent survey, stressed-out women are six times more likely to comfort themselves with junk food than males, while men are more likely to indulge at the local pub when the going gets tough.

But you can limit the effects of stress and boost your body against crippling anxiety by eating a few simple foods. Here, Angela Dowden presents the ultimate guide to the foods and nutrients that fight stress . . .

Carbohydrates
A diet rich in starches and sugars is one of the most effective weapons in fighting the effects of stress, according to a recent Danish study.

When a carbohydrate-rich, protein-poor diet was given to a group of stress-prone 18 to 25-year-olds for a week, they did not show typical signs of depression following a stressful situation.

But when the same group was switched to a diet rich in protein but carbohydrate-poor, they felt more depressed and less vigorous.

According to the study's authors, high-carbohydrate, low-protein foods stimulate the brain's production of the feel-good chemical serotonin and may help anxiety-prone people cope with stressful situations by increasing their level of personal control.

Stress-busters: Bread, potatoes, pasta, rice, noodles, parsnips, carrots, beetroot, bananas, non-diet soft drinks, jam, fruit juice, boiled sweets.

Ginseng
Korean ginseng protects against physical and mental fatigue and provides resistance against stress.

Studies have shown that taken daily, it can increase mental alertness and work output under stressful conditions. It is thought that the herb improves adrenal gland function.

Stress-busters: You should take around 2g of Korean ginseng daily.

Magnesium

Low levels of the mineral magnesium can exacerbate the effects of physical and emotional stress, in particular noise stress.

Loud noises, such as roaring traffic or live music, cause accelerated magnesium loss from cells, accompanied by an increase in calcium and a higher risk of muscle spasms and heart symptoms.

In a recent German study, athletes who consumed extra magnesium showed a reduced negative response to stress without any detrimental effect on performance.

Experts think that keeping up magnesium intake during stress can prevent some of the physical side-effects, such as poor immunity and inflammation.

Stress-busters: Nuts, dried fruit, whole grains, baked beans, kidney beans, lentils, pilchards, sardines, green leafy vegetables.

Vitamin B

The B vitamins are essential for nervous function, and thiamin (vitamin B1) in particular may reduce stress-induced anxiety and improve mood.

In a study of young Welsh women, there was an association between low thiamin levels and feeling less composed, less confident and more depressed. Yet when these women received vitamin supplements for three months, there was a marked improvement in mood in those whose thiamin levels increased.

According to Professor Benton, who carried out the research at the University of Wales in Swansea, about 6% of this Welsh sample of 20-year-olds had thiamin levels so low that their mood was adversely affected.

Stress-busters: Wholegrains, meat, fish, milk, nuts, pulses, peas.

Vitamin C

Large amounts of this vitamin are required by the adrenal glands to make adrenalin, and other stress hormones.

When the body is under stress, vitamin C is used up much faster, and a low intake can weaken the immune system and make it difficult to fight infections or heal wounds.

In endurance runners, daily supplements of 600mg of vitamin C (equivalent to seven oranges) reduced the incidence of stress-induced respiratory tract infection following a competitive race.

Incidence of symptoms was only 33pc in the vitamin C group, compared with 68pc in those who took a placebo. This implies that a diet rich in vitamin C could significantly help you fight stress.

Stress-busters: Oranges and orange juice, green and red peppers, broccoli, Brussels sprouts, guava, cantaloupe melon, strawberries.

Breakfast

Eating a regular breakfast can also make you less stressed.

Studies at Bristol University found that in a range of individuals aged between 20 and 79, those who had breakfast every day perceived themselves as less stressed and suffered less depression and emotional distress compared with those who mostly skipped breakfast.

Breakfast eating was associated with other healthy habits, too, such as not smoking and drinking less

alcohol, but the researchers say that the benefit of breakfast on stress levels was independent of these correlations.

Stress-busters: Nutrient-fortified breakfast cereals such as corn flakes, All Bran and Weetabix had the most significant effect on reducing stress levels, according to the study.

And the foods to avoid

Coffee: Small amounts of caffeine can sharpen your wits, but too much can worsen the stress reaction by stimulating the production of adrenalin, thereby increasing sweating and causing the heart to race, thickening the blood and hormone balance. Stick to no more than four cups of medium-strength coffee a day.

Alcohol: While a couple of glasses of wine can help you de-stress, overdoing it makes matters worse. Like caffeine, alcohol stimulates the heart and can cause shakes and sweating. It also depletes the B vitamins, such as thiamin and B6, which bolster against stress. Safe intakes are no more than two or three units a day for women, and three to four units a day for men.

Chocolate: Studies involving chocaholics have found that it gives only short-lived pleasure and stress relief. In the longer term, stress levels can soar with the feelings of guilt that accompany binge eating.

But moderate chocolate consumption without hang-ups can only make life more tolerable, says the Association For Research into The Science of Enjoyment.

Fizzy drinks: Drinks such as Red Bull contain caffeine and will have the same effect as coffee and tea. They may make you more alert by increasing adrenalin levels, but if drunk in excess they will also make you feel jittery and nervous. While their high sugar levels won't directly exacerbate stress, they increase energy levels and may make it difficult to relax and sleep. Drinks or gum containing the herbal extract gurana can also contribute to stress because it mimics the effects of caffeine.

© *The Daily Mail*
January, 2000

What you can do

Information from ISSUE

When suffering from stress, being confronted with a list of things to do, albeit positive ones, can seem like a pressure in itself. One of the most disconcerting symptoms of stress is the one of feeling out of control and the smallest task can assume monumental proportions. It is a good idea to choose just one or two things from the following list. Set yourself small, realistic goals. The symptoms of stress may take several weeks or months to manifest, unfortunately they rarely disappear overnight. However, taking the initial step of acknowledging that stress is a factor and then deciding to start to address the problem often brings positive results in itself.

Be careful to select the things you really want to do. If the thought of spending a couple of hours doing a yoga class bores you rigid, you will derive little benefit if you are only doing it because you feel you 'ought' to.

If finding time is an issue, then make an appointment with yourself in your diary. If you don't keep it, reschedule it, but, most important of all, don't tell yourself 'well, that's something else I didn't do'. Just tell yourself you will do it next time. Keep giving yourself positive messages to replace the negative ones that are so common when we are stressed.

Anything selected from the following suggestions will help to reduce stress levels:

1. Control your breathing – breathe from the diaphragm, not up in the chest. The deep out-breath is the relaxing one. Breathe in and out through the nose. As you breathe out imagine all the tension and worries melting away.

2. Physical exercise counteracts stress. Swimming, walking and yoga are excellent. Make sure you choose something you really want to do, and try enlisting a friend for moral support.

3. Manage your time more efficiently so that you have time for YOU. List the things you (a) must do, (b) should do and (c) ought to do. Just concentrate on the (a) list and make sure that time for yourself is on the (a) list.

4. Learn to say NO. Being assertive is all about stating your needs, saying something like, 'I have too much on to do X, Y or Z at the moment, but do try asking me again', will get the message over without hurting any feelings.

5. Limit your working hours and work to a schedule.

6. Make goals realistic and attainable.

7. Have a massage – very relaxing. Reflexology or head massage are a good introduction if you are uncertain about a full body massage.

8. Laugh more, sing more, read a light novel. Dancing and painting are great stress relievers, but make sure you do them for the sheer fun of it.

9. Know your limits.

Learn to say NO, saying something like, 'I have too much on to do X, Y or Z at the moment, but do try asking me again'

---

10. Sleep is a good healer. If you can't sleep, get up. Try reading a light book, watching TV, doing light chores, having a milky drink. Limit caffeine intake and don't have any after 4 p.m. Try writing down all your thoughts, worries and things you need to do earlier in the day, so that you are not churning them over at night.

11. Learn to meditate. Join a relaxation class.

12. Learn to 'switch off', control your mind and think positively.

13. There are excellent tapes which will help you to relax. Buy one, familiarise yourself with its technique and then use it before you go to sleep at night.

14. Help is often available from your doctor. Many can refer you to a counsellor for help with stress.

15. Go to your local library and ask for details of courses in stress management and relaxation counselling.

16. There are many good books available in local shops covering stress and how to deal with it. There are also new magazines dealing with health, which may have articles on stress and how to deal with it. Also they tend to have adverts for tapes and videos too.

17. Enlist support from family and friends.

© *ISSUE*

ADDITIONAL RESOURCES

You might like to contact the following organisations for further information. Due to the increasing cost of postage, many organisations cannot respond to enquiries unless they receive a stamped, addressed envelope.

Confederation of British Industry (CBI)
Centre Point
103 New Oxford Street
London, WC1 1DU
Tel: 020 7395 8247
Fax: 020 7240 1578
E-mail: enquiry.desk@cbi.org.uk
Web site: www.cbi.org.uk
Works to ensure that the government of the day, the European Commission and the wider community understand both the needs of British business and the contribution it makes to the well-being of UK society.

The Coronary Prevention Group
2 Taviton Street
London, WC1H 0BT
Tel: 020 7927 2125
Fax: 020 7927 2127
E-mail: cpg@lshtm.ac.uk
Web site: www.healthnet.org.uk
Contributes to the prevention of coronary heart disease, the UK's major cause of death. Provides information to the public on all preventable risk factors – smoking, high blood pressure and raised blood cholesterol and advice on healthy eating, exercise and stress. Produces publications.

The Institute of Management
3rd Floor, 2 Savoy Court
Strand, London, WC2R 0EZ
Tel: 020 7497 0580
Fax: 020 7497 0463
Web site: www.inst-mgt.org.uk
The Institute of Management represents around 86,000 individual managers making it the largest broadly based management institute in the UK.

Institute of Personnel and Development (IPD)
IPD House, Camp Road
Wimbledon
London, SW19 4UX
Tel: 020 8971 9000
Fax: 020 8253 3333

E-mail: ipd@ipd.co.uk
Web site: www.ipd.co.uk
With over 105,000 members it is the professional body for those involved in the management and development of people.

International Stress Management Association (UK)
PO Box 348
Waltham Cross, EN8 8ZL
Tel: 07000 780430
Fax: 01992 426673
E-mail: stress@isma.org.uk
Web site: www.isma.org.uk
ISMA (UK) exists to promote sound knowledge and best practice in the prevention and reduction of human stress. It sets professional standards for the benefit of individuals and organisations using the services of its members.

London Hazards Centre
Interchange Studios
Dalby Street
London, NW5 3NQ
Tel: 020 7267 3387
Fax: 020 7267 3397
E-mail: lonhaz@gn.apc.org
lonhaz@mcr1.poptel.org.uk
Web site: www.lhc.org.uk
The London Hazards Centre runs a free advice service for Londoners, aimed especially at workplace and community groups, health and safety representatives.

Mental Health Foundation
20-21 Cornwall Terrace
London, NW1 4QL
Tel: 020 7535 7400
Fax: 020 7535 7474
E-mail: mhf@mentalhealth.org.uk
Web site: www.mentalhealth.org.uk
Objectives are to prevent mental disorder wherever possible by funding and supporting research and educating people about the causes and effects of stress.

MIND
Granta House, 15-19 Broadway
Stratford, London, E15 4BQ
Tel: 020 8519 2122
Fax: 020 8522 1725
E-mail: contact@mind.org.uk
Web site: www.mind.org.uk
MIND is the leading mental health charity in England and Wales. They produce a wide range of advice leaflets (£1.00 plus A5 sae), reports and books. Helpline 0845 7660163.

PPP healthcare
Phillip House
Crescent Road
Tunbridge Wells, TN1 2PL
Tel: 01892 512345
Fax: 01892 515143
Web site: www.ppphealthcare.co.uk
PPP healthcare is one of the UK's leading private healthcare companies. Health Information Line 0800 003 004.

Royal College of Psychiatrists
17 Belgrave Square
London, SW1X 8PG
Tel: 020 7235 2351
Fax: 020 7235 1935
E-mail: rcpsych@rcpsych.ac.uk
Web site: www.rcpsych.ac.uk
Produces an excellent series of free leaflets on various aspects of mental health. Supplied free of charge but a stamped, addressed envelope is required.

Threshold Women's Mental Health Initiative
14 St George's Place
Brighton, BN1 4GB
Tel: 01273 626444
Fax: 01273 626444
E-mail: thrwomen@globalnet.co.uk
Web site: www.users.globalnet.co.uk/ ~thrwomen
A national information line for women with mental health difficulties. Run for and by women. Provides information on women and mental health, self-help and support groups, counselling and therapy. Information Line tel. 0845 300 0911.

INDEX

absenteeism, and work-related stress 20-1, 26, 27, 28, 29
alcohol consumption, and stress 28, 33, 34, 35, 39
alternative therapies *see* complementary therapies
anti-depressants 7
anxiety
    dealing with stress and 33
    and work-related stress 11, 20
    in young people 6, 7
aromatherapy, and work-related stress 27

breakfasts, eating a regular breakfast 39
breathing exercises 31, 36-7, 40
bullying, and work-related stress 13, 14, 18, 25

caffeine 39
children
    anxiety and phobias in 7
    parents and stress in children 8, 10
    see also young people and stress
chocolate consumption 39
Cognitive Behaviour Therapy (CBT) 17
commuting stress, dealing with 36-7
complementary therapies, for work-related stress 27
cortisol, and exam stress 3
counselling, and work-related stress 20, 26, 28

depression, and work-related stress 11, 20, 28
desk/office rage 26, 30
diet, controlling stress through 31, 35, 38-9
drug abuse
    and anxiety 6
    and stress 18
drug treatments
    for anxiety and phobias 7
    for stress 17

employee assistance programmes 26
employers
    and work-related stress 21, 27
        costs of 14, 19
        legal requirements of 18
    see also managers
exam stress 2, 3-5
    coping with exam results 4
    do's and don'ts 3
    revision tips 5
    stress-busting tips 5
    and suicide 9
exercise, controlling stress through 20, 25, 31, 32-3, 37, 38, 40

ginseng 38-9
GPs (general practitioners), dealing with stress-related illness 28, 33

harassment, and work-related stress 13, 14
health risks, and stress 11, 16, 20, 22, 24, 33
health and safety, and work-related stress 18
heart disease, and stress 20, 34, 35-6

hours of work
    long hours culture 14, 15, 27, 28
        and 'desk rage' 30
        effects on children 10
    and lunch hours 30
    and stress management 32-3

illness
    stress-related 13, 16, 18, 19-20, 22, 28, 30
        see also heart disease

life events, and stress 16, 21-2
lone parents, and stress 34
lunch hours 30

managers
    and office rage 26
    and work-related stress 13, 14-15, 25
        absenteeism 29
    see also employers
massage, controlling stress through 27, 37-8, 40
meditation 38
men, and work-related stress 30
mental health in the workplace 11-12

occupational stress *see* work-related stress
office/desk rage 26, 30
oil rig workers, and stress management 27

parents, and stress in children 8, 10
personality type and stress 16, 22, 32
phobias, in young people 6, 7
post-traumatic stress disorder 6, 18
psychotherapy 7, 17

relaxation
    and anxiety 7
    controlling stress through 17, 20, 25, 31, 33, 35, 36

schools
    stress in school pupils 9-10
        exam stress 2, 3-5, 9
secretarial stress 23-4
self-help
    for controlling stress 17
    groups for anxiety sufferers 7
sleep problems, overcoming insomnia 31, 40
smoking, and stress 30, 33, 35, 36
stress
    avoiding 32-3
    causes of 35
    coping with 31-40
        one-minute stress beaters 36-8
        ten ways to control 27
        work-related stress 13-14, 24
    defining 1
    effects of 1, 16-17
    and personality type 16, 22, 32
    physical responses to 1, 32, 34, 35-6

symptoms of 17, 34
   see also work-related stress; young people and stress
stress-related illness 13, 16, 18, 19-20, 22, 28, 30
   see also heart disease
suicide
   of teachers 10
   and young people 8, 9

technological change, and work-related stress 21, 28
time management 31, 40
tranquillisers 7, 20
type A personality, and stress 16, 32

women
   and stress 34-5
   and stress-related illnesses 20
   and work-related stress 30
work-related stress 11-30
   and absenteeism 20-1, 26, 27, 28, 29
   causes of 18
   collective agreements on 19
   commuting stress 36-7
   costs of 14, 19
   counselling for 20, 26
   dealing with 15
   defining 13, 21
   and desk/office rage 26, 30
   education and awareness 18-19
   effects of 20-1

   group level stress 12
   and illness 13, 16, 18, 19-20, 22, 28, 30
   indicators of 12
   and the individual 12, 19, 21
   legal requirements of employers 18
   and long hours of work 14, 15, 27, 28, 30
   and managers 13, 14-15, 25, 26, 29
   managing 13-14, 24
   and mental health 11-12
      costs of mental ill-health 12
   preventing 22
   research into 14-15, 24
   secretarial stress 23-4
   sources of 13-14, 21-2
   symptoms of 13, 18, 22
   and technological change 21, 28
   and the work environment 24-5

young men, and suicide 8
young people and stress 1-10
   anxiety 6-7
   coping with 1-2
   exam stress 2, 3-5
   getting help 2
   phobias 6, 7
   physical symptoms of 4
   statistics 8
young women, and suicide 8

* * * * *

The Internet has been likened to shopping in a supermarket without aisles. The press of a button on a Web browser can bring up thousands of sites but working your way through them to find what you want can involve long and frustrating on-line searches.

And unfortunately many sites contain inaccurate, misleading or heavily biased information. Our researchers have therefore undertaken an extensive analysis to bring you a selection of quality Web site addresses.

ChildLine

www.childline.org.uk

ChildLine is the UK's free national helpline for children and young people in trouble or danger. Within the Children and Young People section of the web site their are several factsheets on various issues including exam stress and bullying.

The Samaritans

www.samaritans.org.uk

The Samaritans is a nationwide charity which exists to provide confidential emotional support to any person, irrespective of race, creed, age or status. Within the Samaritans web site there is an Exam Stress mini-site. Check out top tips for coping with exam results from Kevin the Teenager and read a letter from Carly Hillman, soap star, on how she coped with her GCSEs last year.

Royal College of Psychiatrists

www.rcpsych.ac.uk

By clicking on Press & Public you can access information within their award-winning series of leaflets *Help is at Hand* or access their mental health factsheets including a factsheet called coping with stress.

International Stress Management Association (UK)

www.isma.org.uk

ISMA (UK) promotes sound knowledge and best practice in the prevention and reduction of human stress. Click on the Articles from Stress News link for a range of relevant information.

Stress UK

www.stress.org.uk

This site is dedicated to education about stress including the following topics: what is stress?, finding personal help, workplace bullying and stress counselling.

ACKNOWLEDGEMENTS

The publisher is grateful for permission to reproduce the following material.

While every care has been taken to trace and acknowledge copyright, the publisher tenders its apology for any accidental infringement or where copyright has proved untraceable. The publisher would be pleased to come to a suitable arrangement in any such case with the rightful owner.

Chapter One: Young People and Stress
Stress, © Royal College of Psychiatrists, *Exams come top of the teenage worry charts*, © The Daily Mail, April 1999, *Top 10 headaches*, © The Daily Mail, April 1999, *Exam stress*, © ChildLine, *Scientists unlock the secret of exam nerves*, © Guardian Newspapers Limited, 2000, *Coping with exam results*, © The Samaritans, *Coping with exam stress*, © International Stress Management Association (UK), *Anxiety and phobias*, © Royal College of Psychiatrists, *Young under more stress*, © Guardian Newspapers Limited, 2000, *Suicide fear for pupils under tests pressure*, © The Independent, April 2000, *Stress, the dos and don'ts*, © Exposure Magazine, *Parents' long hours 'stressing children'*, © Guardian Newspapers Limited, 2000.

Chapter Two: Stress in the Workplace
Mental health in the workplace, © The Mental Health Foundation, *Stress at work*, © Francis Green and Steven McIntosh, *Key facts on stress at work*, © Institute of Personnel and Development, *Taking the strain*, © The Institute of Management, *Stress*, © PPP healthcare, 2000, *Stress at work*, © London Hazards Centre, *Stress a few facts*, © International Stress Management Association (UK), *Stress*, © The Institute of Management, *Wound-up over work*, © Guardian Newspapers Limited, 2000, *Dealing with stress at work*, © MIND, *Our family life is being ruined say stressed bosses*, © The Daily Mail, February 2000, *A problem shared*, © Guardian Newspapers Limited, 2000, *Take it easy, it's only a job*, © The Independent, July 2000, *Off sick with stress*, © The Daily Mail, April 2000, *Half of all workers suffer stress*, © The Independent, April 2000, *Absence cost business £10 billion in 1999 – says survey*, © Confederation of British Industry (CBI), *Rising stress brings 'desk rage' at work*, © Guardian Newspapers Limited, 2000.

Chapter Three: Coping With Stress
Learning to cope with stress, © MIND, *Flora facts – stress*, © By kind permission of Van den Bergh Foods, *Stress and anxiety*, © Mental Health Foundation, *Women and stress*, © Threshold Women & Mental Health Initiative, 2000, *Stress and your heart*, © The Coronary Prevention Group, *One-minute stress beaters*, © The Daily Mail, March 2000, *Eating your stress away*, © The Daily Mail, January 2000, *What you can do*, © ISSUE.

Photographs and illustrations:
Pages 1, 4, 8, 23, 37: Pumpkin House, pages 5, 11, 17, 30, 32, 40: Simon Kneebone.

Craig Donnellan,
Cambridge
September, 2000